DEAR JANE

Dear Jane

A BIOGRAPHICAL STUDY
OF JANE AUSTEN

by

Constance Pilgrim

The Pentland Press Ltd.,
EDINBURGH   CAMBRIDGE   DURHAM

Constance Pilgrim 1971

First published in 1971 by
William Kimber Ltd.

This edition published in 1991 by
The Pentland Press Ltd.
Brockerscliffe
Witton le Wear
Durham

ISBN 1 872795 25 0

Typeset by Print Origination (NW) Ltd., Formby, Liverpool.
Printed and bound by Antony Rowe Ltd., Chippenham.

Jacket design by Geoff Hobbs

823.7 AUS

Contents

The Illustration appearing opposite page 16 is from a painting of a young officer in the uniform of the Royal Engineers (1812–1819)

Our awareness of the family background is also reinforced by scenes presented so vividly that they seem to carry the impress of reality . . . to a large extent this historical content has passed away . . . Its recovery is a task for the historian and biographer.

B. C. SOUTHAM, *Jane Austen's Literary MSS.,*
Oxford University Press, 1964.

Where dark pines framed a silvery sea,
With all sails set, faint thro' the brooding haze,
Like a grey ghost there crept,—O, memory!—
A tall three-masted ship of other days.
I watched as one who knew that her deep hold
Was fraught with treasure, youth's re-captured gold,
Boyhood's delight . . . She bore them, and passed by,
A phantom ship, against a phantom sky.

ALFRED NOYES

Author's Note

I have attempted in this study of Jane Austen, to explore a little known period of her life, the period of 'exquisite felicity,' the meeting with the unknown admirer. It was a time which had the greatest possible influence on the development of her mind.

Her ideal of love—of mind influencing mind—of 'gentleness and fortitude,' of a reciprocal, beneficent development of character, was, for Jane, the only sure foundation of happiness in marriage. That her own happiness ended in tragedy, and her pen was stilled for some years was for her, all part of the maturing process. And if we would but try to follow this growth of her mind, we might find that she has much to say which is helpful to us to-day. For with all our material triumphs, we have lagged lamentably since Jane Austen's day in our progress towards understanding the mind of man, with all its intricate capabilities. We have not yet been able to do more than imagine a world entirely composed of men and women both equally capable of this ideal love. But Jane Austen implies that it existed once.

Direct evidence as to the identity of the unknown gentleman is nowhere forthcoming, so that other methods must be adopted, and nothing is more helpful and fruitful than to turn again to the novels, to re-examine them in depth. If this is done, together with background reading of one kind or another, and much pondering over actual places and scenes described, which may still be visited, we can learn to pick out, to discern, those passages which are descriptive of Jane's actual experience. There may be a few readers who will not be able to accept my identification, but if this is the case, I feel, at any rate, that the young seaman who presented himself at the end of my search, has a very good claim to be Jane Austen's choice.

Introduction

It is well known to admirers of Jane Austen that she experienced a deep and romantic attachment to a man she met while on holiday with her family in the West Country. All evidence as to his identity has been lost, either by the destruction of the relevant letters, or by the confusion of the facts as they were handed down from Jane Austen's sister, Cassandra, to the younger generation of nephews and nieces. Perhaps the remark made by Caroline Austen, James Austen's second daughter, is the safest—that the whole affair can be best described as 'nameless and dateless'. She may well have heard it so described by Cassandra. However that may be, we have the statement of Mrs. Barrett, a friend and admirer of Jane Austen, that Anne Elliot, heroine of *Persuasion* is Jane herself, and from Anne we learn that Jane Austen's lover was a young sailor with his way to make in his career.

Jane Austen's own serious love-story has been dismissed as 'nameless and dateless'—and there it has been allowed to rest for over a hundred and fifty-four years. But members of her family in this century, together with those of her readers who have grown to love her through her novels, have regretted this continued silence. They long to repudiate the ridiculous suggestion made by some critics of her letters that they reveal her as a colourless spinster. They feel that the spontaneous opinions expressed by her nephews and nieces, young as they were at her death, reveal a nature full of sweetness, joy, unselfishness, and unfailing good-humour. So there is a gap to be filled.

Introduction

Mary Augusta Austen-Leigh, a great niece, wrote in 1920: 'Not only, therefore, in quantity, these letters are entirely unworthy specimens of her correspondence in general. They are but "a gleaning of grapes when the vintage is done—" when all that was precious had been safely gathered up, and garnered in Cassandra's faithful memory, and nothing remained excepting that which even she deemed to be altogether negligible. How vain, then, must be any attempt to extract from this unvalued remainder that wine of the spirit with which all the spontaneous and uncensored works of Jane Austen's imaginative soul are richly filled.'

As we turn again to the novels, and re-read them, our step falls into place with her own, our ear becomes keener, and we gradually, imperceptibly, are made aware of those passages in her novels—which are 'presented so vividly that they seem to carry the impress of reality . . .' These are the experiences which Jane 'felt on her pulses.'

1. Jane Austen: A Biographical Sketch

I can indeed bear witness that there was
scarcely a charm in her most delightful
characters that was not a true reflection of
her own sweet temper and loving heart.

J. E. AUSTEN-LEIGH, *Memoir*.

An iron tethering ring, worn thin with age and use, let into
an old stone wall that skirts the desolate and forsaken garden.
Where once were shrubs and a planted approach are now
wild flowers and a grassy plot, backed by a sheer rock surface;
in a cleft a stream can be heard trickling downwards to run
into a wild part of the former garden, now overgrown with
dank reeds, bog iris, nettles. Above overhang sapling timber,
self-sown, wild and luxuriant. High above yellow gorse covers
part of St. Boniface Down. The house has long since gone—
'That sweet St. Bon [iface House] ...'[1] Some say it was haunted.
But the tethering ring remains, evocative—mysterious.

What was the mystery in Jane Austen's life? Two periods
of literary activity—the first in her youth, the second in her
late thirties—separated by ten or more years of suppressed
talent, gifts held in check, an arid period. Why? Was it the
disruption of the secure country family life when their father,
the Reverend George Austen, left his rectory at Steventon,
handing the parish over to his eldest son, James Austen, and
retiring to Bath in 1801? Or was this upheaval but an
aggravation of a deeper unhappiness—the tearing apart of
Jane and her elusive lover, the hero of the West Country
romance? It will be as well to examine the different versions

11

of this story which have been handed down to us, but first a brief biography of Jane Austen herself is necessary.

Jane Austen was born at Steventon Rectory, Hampshire on December 16th, 1775. Her father was the Reverend George Austen (1731–1805), a son of William Austen, a surgeon of Tonbridge, Kent. George Austen was orphaned early—and was befriended by an uncle, Francis Austen, who sent him to the school at Tonbridge, and from there he became a scholar of St. John's College, Oxford. He later became a fellow of his college—and being ordained, was presented to the living of Steventon, Hampshire in 1761, by his kinsman, Thomas Knight, of Godmersham, Kent. Later, in 1773 he obtained the living of Deane, only a mile away from Steventon, this living being bought for him by his uncle Francis. 'This was no very gross case of plurality, according to the ideas of that time, for the two villages were little more than a mile apart, and their united populations scarcely amounted to 300.'[2]

The Reverend George Austen remained at Steventon all his working life, marrying Cassandra Leigh in 1764. She was the daughter of Thomas Leigh of Adlestrop, Gloucester; a younger branch were at Stoneleigh, Warwicks. Her father was a fellow of All Souls, Oxford, and held the college living of Harpsden, near Henley. One of Cassandra Leigh's uncles was Theophilus Leigh, Master of Balliol, Oxford, and another was father and grandfather of the two Leighs who succeeded to the Stoneleigh estates. George and Cassandra Austen had six sons and two daughters. In order to augment his stipend, and provide for his growing family, George Austen took pupils into his house, educating his sons as well, until they were ready for the university.[3] 'With his sons (all promising to make figures in life), Mr. Austen educates a few youths of chosen friends and acquaintances. When among this liberal society, the simplicity, hospitality and taste which commonly prevail in similar families among the delightful valleys of Switzerland ever recur.'

Jane, at the age of seven accompanied her only sister Cassandra her senior by two years, to boarding school—first to a Mrs. Cawley, whose school was first at Oxford, and later to Southampton, during which time Jane nearly died of a fever. Then for two years the girls were at the Abbey School, Reading. Thereafter they too were educated at home. From that date until Mr. Austen left Steventon and retired to live at Bath in 1801, Jane Austen's life continued to be governed by the normal day to day happenings of a large and happy family. Brought up in a country rectory, with only a moderate income, all were industrious.

From 1799, when the move to Bath was first projected (the Austens settled at Bath in the autumn of 1801), until 1809 when Mrs. Austen, now widowed, returned to make her home with her two daughters in their beloved Hampshire again at Chawton, Jane Austen's life had been unsettled. It is therefore not surprising that most of her literary critics have attributed her so-called arid period to the distraction of having no really settled home.

To value Jane Austen's novels as they should be valued, we have to know about their creator. Some people think of her as utterly unromantic, unpoetical—they mistakenly feel that her main concern is with comedy. But others feel she has a sensitive, delicate and perceptive understanding of man in his human predicament which is loving and balanced; portraying him in the 'round', revealing his deep spiritual qualities, and his human frailities. Her love of nature in all her books is utterly fresh and truly poetical. It should be remembered, though at first sight it may seem incongruous, that almost her last word is to remind us that 'Wordsworth has the true soul of Poetry'—thus showing her appreciation of that greatest and most deeply observant of our nature poets; she shows a developing interest in his work.

What we have to do about Jane Austen is to rid ourselves

of the completely false notions about her which have grown
up and hardened into a quite grossly inaccurate image. This
is beginning to split up under the pressure of recent critical
judgements and re-appraisals. The source of one of the false
pictures may no doubt be traced to the description given to
Miss Mitford by a friend.

'She [Jane Austen] has stiffened into the most perpendicu-
lar, precise, taciturn piece of single-blessedness.'

This source was said to be 'poisoned'—as the friend of Miss
Mitford was being sued by Edward Knight (Jane's brother) at
this time.

But this untrue picture of Jane Austen is also due in great
part to looking at her life through the wrong end of the
telescope, taking the impressions of her younger relatives as
they knew her: sweet and kind though they remembered her,
still, it was towards the *end* of her life, when she was failing
in health, at Chawton. They knew nothing of the warm,
passionate girl of Steventon days; they could not imagine her,
the pale, fragile woman in the donkey-carriage—what had
she to do with the warm, richly colourful girl? Brilliant and
attractive, apt pupil of her father, and scholarly brother,
James: going far beyond him in her abilities, and often a
companion on his rambles, and at his London parties; of the
witty handsome brother, Henry. Walking and riding in the
Hampshire countryside with Cassandra or Martha Lloyd,
dancing at the balls of the local families, or at the assembly
rooms, visiting Bath and London, Kent or the sea—all this led
her to her one real romance. It would have been quite impossible for the younger generation of nephews and nieces to
visualise the lovely, vivacious girl their Aunt Jane had once
been. Only Edward, James' son, came nearest to such a
realisation in his poem of boyhood days.[4]

2. Romance

The nameless and dateless lover.

Jane Austen is known, as we have seen, to have had one serious love story in her life. There are at least five separate versions of the story, and they all derive, ultimately, from Cassandra, her sister. One, repeated by Mrs. Bellas, seems to have more coherence than the other versions. This maybe because it comes from Mrs. Bellas's mother, Jane Anna Elizabeth, James Austen's eldest child, later Mrs. Benjamin Lefroy. She was Jane's first niece, and was closest to her, in many ways, and certainly loved and admired her aunt profoundly. There is a strong possibility that this version came direct from Jane herself to Anna, as well as through her aunt Cassandra. Anna told the story to her half-brother, James Edward Austen-Leigh, at the time he was collecting material for his *Memoir* of his aunt, and her daughter, Mrs. Bellas, wrote the story down:

'The Austens with their two daughters were once at Teignmouth, the date of that visit was not later than 1802, but besides this they were once travelling in Devonshire, moving about from place to place, and I think that tour was before they left Steventon in 1801, perhaps as early as 1798 or 1799. It was while they were so travelling, according to Aunt Cassandra's account many years afterwards, that they somehow made acquaintance with a gentleman of the name of Blackall. He and Aunt Jane mutually attracted each other, and such was his charm that even Aunt Cassandra thought

15

him worthy of her sister. They parted on the understanding that he was to come to Steventon, but instead came I know not how long after a letter from his brother to say that he was dead.

'There is no record of Jane's affliction, but I think this attachment must have been very deep. Aunt Cassandra herself had so warm a regard for him that some years after her sister's death, she took a good deal of trouble to find out and see again his brother. Extract of a letter from our dear Aunt Caroline [Anna Lefroy's half-sister], to Mary Augusta Austen-Leigh:

"I have no doubt that Aunt Jane was beloved of several in the course of her life and was herself very capable of loving. I wish I could give you more dates as to Mr. Blackall. All that I know is this. At Newtown Aunt Cassandra was staying with us when we made the acquaintance of a certain Mr. Henry Eldridge of the Engineers. He was very pleasing and very good looking. My Aunt was much struck with him, and I was struck by her commendation as she rarely admired anyone. Afterwards she spoke of him as one so unusually gifted with all that was agreeable, and said he had reminded her strongly of a gentleman whom they had met one summer when they were by the sea (I think she said in Devonshire) who had seemed greatly attracted by my Aunt Jane. That when they parted (I imagine he was a visitor there also, but his family might have lived near) he was urgent to know where they would be next summer, implying or perhaps saying that he should be there also wherever it might be. I can only say that the impression left on Aunt Cassandra's mind was that he had fallen in love with Aunt Jane. Soon afterwards they heard of his death. I am sure she thought him worthy of her sister from the way she recalled his memory, and also that she did not doubt either that he would have been a successful suitor." '

An officer in The Royal Engineers, in the full dress coat worn between 1812 and 1819. There is evidence that the portrait may be of Mr. Henry Thomas Edridge. For a full note see page 172.

These two versions are inconsistent, as Mrs. Bellas's statement that the suitor was expected at Steventon does not correspond with that part of Caroline's letter. There is also another account by Caroline Austen, which she sent to her brother at the time he was compiling his material for the *Memoir;* she writes:

'During the few years my grandfather lived at Bath, he went in the summer with his wife and daughters to some seaside. They were in Devonshire, and in Wales—and in Devonshire an acquaintance was made with some very charming man—I never heard Aunt Cassandra speak of anyone else with such admiration—she had no doubt that a mutual attachment was in progress between him and her sister. They parted—but he made it plain that he should seek them out again—and shortly afterwards he died. My Aunt told me this in late years of her own life, and it was quite new to me then, but all this, being nameless and dateless, cannot I know, serve any purpose of yours—and it brings no contradiction to your theory that Aunt Jane never had any attachment that overclouded her happiness, for long. This had not gone far enough to leave misery behind.'

Again there are inconsistencies, for 'nameless and dateless' contradicts the statement in the earlier letter that the lover's name was Blackall. There is also a marked discrepancy in the effect on Jane's happiness. There is a letter from Mrs. Hubback (Francis Austen's daughter, Caroline), the main point of which is to dispense with Mr. Blackall, as she remembers Aunt Cassandra meeting him in 1832 (long after Jane Austen's death) and finding him 'stout, red-faced and middle-aged'.

There is a note in Mrs. Bellas's copy of the *Brabourne Letters:*

'In the summer of 1801 the father, mother and daughters made a tour in Devonshire. They went to Teignmouth, Starcross, Sidmouth, etc. I believe it was at the last named place that they made acquaintance with a young clergyman when visiting his brother, who was one of the doctors of the town. He and Jane fell in love with each other, and when the Austens left he asked to be allowed to join them again further on in their tour, and the permission was given. But instead of his arriving as expected, they received a letter announcing his death. In Aunt Cassandra's memory he lived as one of the most charming persons she had known, worthy even in her eyes of Aunt Jane.'

James Edward gathers the different stories together, and produces his own version in the *Memoir* of 1870: 'There is one passage of romance in her history with which I am imperfectly acquainted, and to which I am unable to assign name, or date, or place, though I have it on sufficient authority. Many years after her death, some circumstances induced her sister Cassandra to break through her habitual reticence, and to speak of it. She said that while staying at some seaside place, they became acquainted with a gentleman, whose charm of person, mind and manners was such that Cassandra thought him worthy to possess and likely to win her sister's love. When they parted, he expressed his intention of soon seeing them again; and Cassandra felt no doubt as to his motives. But they never again met. Within a short time they heard of his sudden death. I believe that, if Jane ever loved, it was this unnamed gentleman; but the acquaintance had been short, and I am unable to say whether her feelings were of such a nature as to affect her happiness.'

These versions of the story of Jane Austen's mysterious romance are all that have come down to us. The information they give is not enough to make identification of the hero of them at all possible, and so we must turn to the novels to find him. But before doing so there are two other clues apart from the letters; the first, the testimony of her friend, the unknown Mrs. Barrett. Chapman accepts her evidence as valid, saying:

'We do not know who Mrs. Barrett was, nor the degree of her acquaintance with Jane, but she is obviously a good witness. Austen-Leigh was entitled to accept her evidence. We are bound to do the same.'[1]

Mrs. Barrett, in her tribute to Jane which Austen-Leigh recollects in his *Memoir*, says: 'Anne Elliot *was* herself; her enthusiasm for the navy, and her perfect unselfishness, reflect her completely.' And there is one other scrap of evidence—although the authors of the *Life and Letters* discounted it.

'A story is given in the *Reminiscences of Sir Francis H. Doyle*, to the effect that Mr. Austen, accompanied by Cassandra and Jane, took advantage of the Peace of Amiens, in 1802, to undertake a foreign tour. Whilst in Switzerland, they fell in with a young naval officer, who speedily became attached to Jane. His love was returned, and all seemed to be going smoothly. The party were making for Chamonix; but while the Austens kept to such high road as there was, their friend was to make his way thither over the mountains. The Austens reached Chamonix safely, but their friend never arrived, and at last news came that he had over-tired himself and died of a brain fever on the way. The Austens returned to England, and Jane resumed her ordinary life, never referring to her adventures abroad.'

This story is discounted for three reasons, that such an important event as a tour abroad would have left some trace, secondly that Mr. Austen could not possibly have afforded it. He had given up his living, and was hoping to have £600 a year as the most he could expect, for the four of them to live on in Bath. Thirdly, they are known to have been on holiday in Dawlish, South Devon, sometime in 1802. However, the story, in the main, resembles the other accounts, and at one point seems to be less confused—namely, the fact that the hero is a naval officer. This coincides exactly with Mrs. Barrett's identification of Anne Elliot with Jane herself, and leads us to Captain Wentworth, the naval officer, hero of *Persuasion*, and Anne's lover.

'Captain Frederick Wentworth being made Commander in the summer of 1806, having no parent living and not being immediately employed, made his home for half a year, with his brother, in Somersetshire.'

At this period he is described as: 'A remarkably fine young man, with a great deal of intelligence, spirit and brilliancy.'

We are told that he 'had no fortune. He had been lucky in his profession, but spending freely, what had come freely, had realised nothing. But he was confident that he should soon be rich—full of life and ardour, he knew that he should soon have a ship, and soon be on a station that would lead to everything he wanted.'

Lady Russell, Anne's friend, disapproved of Captain Wentworth as Anne's lover on the grounds of the imprudence of a marriage between them—they are both too poor. He and Anne are forced to part: 'The belief of being prudent and self-denying principally for his advantage, was her chief consolation, under the misery of parting—a final parting and every consolation was required, for she had to encounter all the additional pain of opinions, on his side, totally unconvinced and unbending, and of his feeling himself ill-used by so forced a relinquishment.' Seven years later, Captain Wentworth re-appears in the same Somersetshire circle as Anne's— this time coming to stay with his married sister, who with her husband, Admiral Croft, are tenants of Anne's father, Sir Walter Elliot, of their old home, Kellynch Hall. Captain Wentworth, ignoring Anne, attempts friendship with the Musgrove girls. They show a keen interest in his naval career —and they begin to pore over the Navy Lists—to find 'out the ships which Captain Wentworth had commanded'.

' "Your first was the *Asp*, I remember; we will look for the *Asp*."

' "You will not find her there. Quite worn out and broken up. I was the last man who commanded her. Hardly fit for service then. Reported fit for home waters for a year or two, and so I was sent off to the West Indies."

'The girls looked all amazement.

' "The Admiralty," he continued, "entertain themselves now and then, with sending a few hundred men to sea, in a ship not fit to be employed. But they have a great many to provide for; and among the thousands that may just as well go to the bottom as not, it is impossible for them to distinguish the very set who may be least missed." ' But Admiral Croft, Captain Wentworth's brother-in-law, will have none of this:

' "Phoo! Phoo!" cried the Admiral, "what stuff these young fellows talk! Never was a better sloop than the *Asp* in her day. For an old built sloop, you would not see her equal. Lucky fellow to get her! He knows there must have been twenty better men than himself applying for her at the same time. Lucky fellow to get anything so soon, with no more interest than his."

' "I felt my luck, Admiral, I assure you;" replied Captain Wentworth, seriously. "I was as well satisfied with my appointment as you can desire. It was a great object with me at that time, to be at sea, a very great object. I wanted to be doing something." ' The Admiral's comment is to agree, saying, that what should a young fellow like Captain Wentworth do ashore for half a year together? ' "If a man has not a wife, he soon wants to be afloat again." '

Captain Wentworth then describes his ship to Louisa and Henrietta Musgrove, telling of the *Asp's* age, her condition, and his last voyage in her:

' "I had no more discoveries to make, than you would have as to the fashion and strength of any old pelisse which you had seen lent about among half your acquaintance, ever since you could remember, and which at last, on some very wet day, is lent to yourself. Ah! She was a dear old *Asp* to me. She did all that I wanted. I knew she would. I knew that we should either go to the bottom together, or that she would be the making of me; and I never had two days of foul weather all the time I was at sea in her; and after taking privateers enough to be very entertaining, I had the good luck, in my passage home the next autumn, to fall in with the very French frigate I wanted.—I brought her into Plymouth; and here was another instance of luck. We had not been six hours in the Sound, when a gale came on, which lasted four days and nights, and which would have done for poor old *Asp*, in half the time; our touch with the Great Nation not having much improved our condition. Four and twenty hours later, and I should only have been a gallant Captain Wentworth, in a small paragraph at one corner of the newspapers; and being lost in only a sloop, nobody would have thought about me."

'Anne's shudderings were to herself alone.'

3. Shipwreck

O 'tis a passionate work!—yet wise and well,
Well chosen is the spirit that is here;
That Hulk which labours in the deadly swell,
This rueful sky, this pageantry of fear!

WILLIAM WORDSWORTH, Elegaic stanzas
suggested by a picture of Peele Castle.

On January 23rd, 1805,[1] Captain John Wordsworth, of the
East Indiaman, *The Earl of Abergavenny*, writes to his cousin,
Captain Wordsworth that he has arrived at Portsmouth, and
is waiting there for a favourable wind to set out on his third
voyage as the ship's commander. He writes again to his cousin
on the 31st, telling him: 'The Commodore intends to go
through The Needles, a passage I do not like much but I hope
will be attended with no accident.'

In the first days of February, he put to sea. All went well
until February 5th, when, just off Portland Bill, the *Abergavenny* ran into a westerly gale. The story is told in a copy
of Thomas Gilpin's Memorandum, delivered to the East India
Court of Directors, and sent by Charles Lamb, a friend of the
Wordsworths, to them:

'Thomas Gilpin (1st Mate of the ship)
'At 10 a.m. being about ten leagues to the westward of
Portland, the Commodore made the signal to bear up—did so
accordingly; at this time having maintop gallant mast struck,
fore and mizen do. on deck, and the jib boom in the wind
about W.S.W. At 3 p.m. got on board a pilot, being about 2

leagues to the westward of Portland; ranged and bitted both cables at about ½ past 3, called all hands and got out the jib boom at about 4. While crossing the east end of the Shambles, the wind suddenly died away, and a strong tide setting the ship to the westward, drifted her into the breakers, and a sea striking her on the larboard quarter, brought her to, with her head to the northward, when she instantly struck, it being about 5 p.m. Let out all the reefs, and hoisted the topsails up, in hopes to shoot the ship across the Shambles. About this time the wind shifted to the N.W. The surf driving us off, and the tide setting us on alternately, sometimes having 4½ at others 9 fathoms, sand of the sea about 8 feet; continued in this situation till about ½ past 7, when she got off. During the time she was on the Shambles, had from 3 to 4 feet water; kept the water at this height about 15 minutes, during the whole time the pumps constantly going. Finding she gained on us, it was determined to run her on the nearest shore. About 8 the wind shifted to the eastward; the leak continuing to gain upon the pumps, having 10 or 11 feet water, found it expedient to bale at the forescuttles and hatchway. The ship would not bear up—kept the helm hard a starboard, she being water-logg'd: but still had a hope she could be kept up till we got her on Weymouth Sands. Cut the lashings of the boats—could not get the long boat out, without laying the main-top-sail aback, by which our progress would have been delayed, that no hope would have been left us of running her aground, and there being several sloops in sight, one having sent a small skiff on board, took away two ladies and three other passengers, and put them on board the sloop, at the same time promising to return and take away a hundred or more of the people: she finding much difficulty in getting back to the sloop, did not return. About this time the Third Mate and Purser were sent in the cutter to get assistance from the other ships. Continued pumping and baling till 11 p.m.

when she sunk. Last cast of the lead 11 fathoms. Having fired guns from the time she struck till she went down; about 2 a.m. boats came and took the people from the wreck about seventy in number. The troops, in particular The Dragoons pumped very well.

[Signed] Thos' Gilpin.'²

This account of the disastrous sinking of *The Earl of Abergavenny* with over half the people drowned and her entire cargo lost, is as accurate as possible. It does not, because of the bare, simple language used, give any idea of the terrible night it must have been, with a rising storm, the hectic pumping and baling, as the water-logged vessel gradually sank, the atmosphere of horror, the roar of the wind and the grinding fury of the current as the ship was forced on and off the Shambles, the men now hoping, now fearing that they would or would not, reach the safety of Weymouth Sands. But it was not to be; the great ship went down, and with her died her gallant, much beloved Commander, Captain John Wordsworth. They found him, six weeks later, beside the wreck of his ship. And so, instead of returning, after a successful voyage, to lead a peaceful life in the Vale of Grasmere with those he loved, he became 'only a gallant Captain Wordsworth' in a paragraph in the newspapers.

We saw in the last chapter how Jane Austen and Anne Elliot are one person. We know that the story of *Persuasion* contains a great deal of material that is autobiographical. So it will be useful to cast about and see if there may not be a young seaman, contemporary with Jane Austen, who may have some, at any rate, of the same qualities and qualifications, as Captain Wentworth, and also someone the Austen family could have known, personally.

There is such a young man, who fits the role to perfection, and his name is John Wordsworth, the poet's younger brother, Commander of *The Earl of Abergavenny*, whose death by drowning, as we have seen above, occurred on February 5th, 1805.

John Wordsworth was born on December 4th, 1772, the third of John and Anne Wordsworth's four sons, at Cockermouth, in the 17th century, long shaped house which his father occupied as the steward of Sir James Lowther. The house stands near the bridge over the Derwent, the river running along the garden at the back. The Wordsworth children, Richard, William, Dorothy, John and Christopher loved this garden, with its high terrace, and its riverside meadows, which were another favourite haunt.

They lost their mother in 1778, when they were all too young for such a blow. Their father was pre-occupied with his duties as manager of the Lowther estates, and also with other local public offices and it was inevitable that he should have little time for his children. He was a reserved man, devoted to the wife he had lost and an affectionate brother and brother-in-law. His eloquence, mental vigour and honesty caused him to be much respected amongst his neighbours.

'William owed his father one great debt. He cared for English poetry, and it was he who taught his son to learn by heart "large portions of Shakespeare, Milton and Spenser."[3] His library was at his sons' disposal at all times;' and this library bears witness to his literary tastes and interests. It has been noted that he was not, perhaps, the type of man who finds it easy to enter into the hopes and plans of his children. Yet William Wordsworth, writing to his friend, James Losh, a month after the death of his brother John in 1805, quotes his father as saying, of his son John, 'He used to call him Ibex, the shyest of all the beasts,' which surely points to a knowledge of the boy's disposition, based on close sympathy and understanding.

The Wordsworth children lost their father in 1783, and

the boys were left in the care of their maternal grandparents
—William Cookson, mercer of Penrith, and his wife,
Dorothy, formerly Crackanthorpe, heiress of Newbiggin
Hall. They were not at all suited to bring up such young
children.

John was educated with his brothers at Hawkshead Gram-
mar School. (Dorothy, their only sister, was cared for at
Halifax by her mother's cousin, Elizabeth Threlkeld.) He left
school at Christmas, 1787; William had left in the October of
that year to go on to Cambridge and John spent the next year
partly with his Uncle Richard Wordsworth, at Whitehaven.
He studied navigation under a Mr. Wood for a short time,
and then served in various trading vessels from Whitehaven.

It is not certain when the decision was made for John to
enter upon a career at sea. He entered the East India Company
in 1790, sailing in *The Earl of Abergavenny* under the command of his older cousin, Captain John Wordsworth, son of
his Uncle Richard of Whitehaven, whose interest, and that
of John Robinson (M.P. for Harwich), a cousin of John's
father, had obtained the boy's entry into the service.

The complete unselfishness of his nature is reflected in a
letter of his sister Dorothy, written in 1787 from Penrith to
her friend of childhood days at Halifax, Jane Pollard.

'We shall, however, have sufficient to educate my brothers.
John, poor fellow! says that he shall have occasion for very
little—£200 will be enough to fit him out and he should wish
William to have the rest for *his* education, as he wishes to be
a lawyer, if his health will permit, and it will be very
expensive.'

All the boys were taught to ride and to dance; and among
the children of the north country families with whom the
Wordsworth boys and their sister were friendly, were the
Speddings of Armathwaite Hall, an estate which had been

bought by their grandfather at the foot of Bassenthwaite. John Spedding had been a schoolfellow at Hawkshead, and his mother and sisters, Maria and Margaret, high spirited and lively girls, were always pleased to welcome the Wordsworths whenever they visited them.

John Wordsworth began his career at sea early in 1788; a letter of Dorothy, to her friend Jane Pollard in January of that year, reads, 'My brother John has set sail for Barbadoes. I hope poor lad! that he will be successful and happy, he is much delighted with the profession he has chosen. How we are squandered abroad!'

John returned from these voyages in the spring of 1789, and sailed again January 1790, bound for India, in the East Indiaman, *The Abergavenny*, then commanded by his cousin, Captain Wordsworth, senior. He had spent the Christmas holidays with William, who had come up from Cambridge to be with him before he sailed in the New Year.

We must suppose that from now on John spent his time between voyages in several places; sometimes with his uncle Richard's family at Whitehaven or at Newcastle with the Griffith family of cousins, or at Forncett Rectory, Hertfordshire, with his maternal uncle, Canon Cookson and his wife (Dorothy lived there from 1788 till 1794) or in London, chiefly using his brother Richard's chambers, Staple Inn, as his headquarters. He may possibly have stayed occasionally at Wyke House, Syon Hill, the home of his father's influential cousin, John Robinson. After Mr. Wordsworth's death, John Robinson was always kind to all the Wordsworth children, and would have welcomed John at his Isleworth home. There must also have been unrecorded visits to friends of his own, and colleagues, in other parts of the country. In October 1791 Dorothy writes, 'My brother John is arrived in England, and I am told is grown a tall, handsome man. I hope we shall see him at Forncett ere long.'

In the spring John arrived at Forncett Rectory and stayed for some months, then going to London, en route for the north, hoping to sail again from Whitehaven. Before doing so, he visited his mother's cousins, the Misses Griffith, at Newcastle for a few days, and then on to Penrith, to see his grandmother, Mrs. Cookson, now a widow. In a letter to her brother Richard, Dorothy says, 'I have received a letter from John today written the day after his safe arrival at Penrith, where he found my Grandmother better than she has been for some time.' However, it must have been a temporary recovery, for Grandmother Cookson died in June 1792.

In August 1793 Dorothy writes, 'John, poor dear fellow! is on his road to the East Indies;' there is no further news of him in her letters till January 1795 when she writes to her brother Richard Wordsworth, from Newcastle (where she is staying with the Griffith cousins, on a visit after her sojourn with William at Windy Brow, the home of his friends, the Calvert brothers), and says, 'It is very long since I heard from John, pray tell him I have written to him twice since I heard from him: the first time I directed my letter to Staple Inn and the second to Gravesend. I should suppose he will be thinking about going to Forncett now. You will consult together about the propriety of his taking my £100 out, with him, to which I give my consent in case you approve of it.'

The next mention of John is in a letter of Dorothy to her friend Jane Pollard (now Mrs. Marshall—she married in August 1795) written on September 2nd, 1795, when the 'Racedown' plan is talked of for the first time. She writes:

'Kitt is very much pleased with the plan; it will indeed be a great comfort to him and John to have a place to draw to and I hope we shall oftener meet than we have ever hitherto had it in our power.'

Of Racedown, Dorset, the house let to Dorothy and her brother William by the Pinney family, she says, 'If you want to find our situation out, look in your maps for Crewkerne, Chard, Axminster, Bridport and Lime; we are nearly equidistant from all those places.' There may very well have been an unrecorded visit of John Wordsworth's to Racedown. We hear nothing of him again, from his sister, until April 30th, 1798, when she writes to Richard from Alfoxden, in the north of the county of Somerset, 'I was very glad to hear so good an account of poor John. When is he expected home again? I wish we could see you here before we go. You would be delighted with this place. William sends his love to you.'

On August 20th, 1799, Dorothy writes to Richard from Sockburn, in Yorkshire, the home of Thomas, George and Mary Hutchinson, where she is staying with William after returning from a German tour. 'I have for some time expected impatiently to hear of John's arrival in England—pray let us know as soon as you hear of him. God bless you!' She writes again on September 3rd, 'The day after William's letter to you was sent off we heard of John's arrival in England, but no particulars; we have since anxiously expected news of him.'

John had arrived back in England from an East Indian voyage in August 1799—and came up North to attend the funeral of his Uncle Christopher Crackanthorpe, of Newbiggin Hall. In October he joined William and Coleridge on a walking tour from Temple Sowerby, going by way of Haweswater, Bowness and Hawkshead, reaching Grasmere, where they stayed at Robert Newton's Inn. John probably returned to Newbiggin—and William, writing to Dorothy, says, 'You will think my plan a mad one, but I have thought of building a house there [at Grasmere] by the lake side. John would give me £40 to buy the ground . . . there is a small house at Grasmere empty, which we might take, but of this we will speak.'

It was Dove Cottage. William and Dorothy moved in on

December 20th, 1799, and in a letter to Coleridge, dated Christmas Eve, he says: 'We are looking for John every day.' John came, and stayed till September 1800 on leave while waiting to be sworn in as the new Commander of the Indiaman he had already served on, *The Earl of Abergavenny*, in succession to his cousin, Captain John Wordsworth senior.

When the great Indiaman reached England again, John returned to London, staying a while at Forncett with his Uncle and Aunt Cookson, on his way south. While waiting about in London, he was employed by William to see the second edition of the *Lyrical Ballads* through the press. The other side of this shy, reserved 'natural poet', is revealed in some of his letters at this time; some are to Mary Hutchinson with whom he had become very friendly when she came to stay during his Grasmere sojourn in 1800. They are full of glowing enthusiasm for much of William's poetry—and great indignation at the profits to be made by Longman from the edition, and the slothfulness of their progress towards publication.

John sailed at last from Portsmouth in May 1801, his first voyage as the ship's Commander. He was back in August, 1802, and there is a happy family reunion with all his brothers and Dorothy in Richard's chambers, for William and Dorothy, having seized the chance of the Peace of Amiens, March 1802, to make a quick trip to Calais to visit Annette and Caroline, Wordsworth's daughter, were just recently returned. Christopher came up from Cambridge to join them all, and there is a charming description of John's appearance, in a letter from Dorothy to Mary Hutchinson, dated September 12th, (or 19th) 1802:

'We returned from Windsor yesterday evening and repaired immediately to Staple Inn where we were informed by Richard's clerk that our dear John was arrived and in perfect health. We hastened towards our own lodging and just as we entered Temple Court we met Richard and John who were walking backwards and forwards by the light of the moon and the lamps. I could just see enough of John to know that he looked uncommonly well, and when we got him into Paper Buildings and had lighted the candles I saw that he was grown fat and looked very handsome.'

John Wordsworth did not sail again on his second voyage as *The Earl of Abergavenny's* Commander until May 1803. So he was able to send a gift to Mary Hutchinson for her wedding to William on October 9th at Wyke, Scarborough. He sailed in May 1803, and was away until August 1804. This voyage had been a little more profitable to him and he had enough to invest in his next voyage, but it had also been more eventful than the earlier voyage. For on the return voyage the China Fleet of East Indiamen ran into a French Squadron under Admiral Linois. Some fighting occurred, but eventually the French were beaten off and the fleet reached Malacca in safety.

It is possible that, in the opinion of some people, this en-counter with the French—'this touch with the Great Nation' —had not very much improved the condition, of some at least, of the Indiamen. And although John Wordsworth, writing from his ship to his cousin, Captain Wordsworth, senior, on his return up the channel on August 8th, 1804, reports that the *Abergavenny* has 'no damage of any description and that the ship has suffered as little as if she had remained in Mr. Pitcher's dock for the time she has been out', Jane Austen is no doubt using 'poetic licence' when she attributes the sink-ing of the *Asp* in *Persuasion* to her 'touch with the Great Nation'.

At the start of her third voyage early in 1805, a gale came on which lasted for a considerable time. The great ship *The Earl of Abergavenny* was unable to stand up to the savage pounding of wind and sea, and rapidly becoming water-logged sank 'in half the time' tragically near the safety of Weymouth Bay. Some observers of the day would perhaps have attributed this also to the encounter with the French, endured by all the ships of the China Fleet, at their gallant defeat of Admiral Linois's Squadron.

4. Biographical Evidence in the Novels and other Sources

A Chaise was sent for from Crewkerne.

JANE AUSTEN, *Persuasion*.

'A chaise was sent for from Crewkerne.' This information is given in *Persuasion*; the chaise was needed to convey an old family nurse, Sarah, to Lyme from Uppercross, to help Louisa Musgrove, lying ill of a concussion at Captain and Mrs. Harville's cottage at Lyme, caused by her ill-advised jump down the steps on the Cobb, and her consequent fall.

Crewkerne is the nearest market town to Uppercross—Kellynch Hall is said to be three miles away, and Lyme seventeen. It is generally agreed that in *Persuasion* Jane Austen is describing a countryside she knew and had visited. It comes very near to the countryside of Racedown (the Wordsworths' home from 1795–1797), just over the border into Dorset, on the Crewkerne Lyme road, and visible from the upper windows of 'a sizeable Jacobean manor of pink sandstone'[1] which almost certainly suggested Kellynch Hall, Anne Elliot's home. This house, just inside the Somerset border would have an especial appeal to Jane Austen, connected as its name is with her Mother's family, who, like Sir Walter Elliot's, originally came from Cheshire.

When John returned to England in the early spring of 1797, there would not have been time for him to visit William and Dorothy at Racedown in February, for he was almost immediately re-employed on another vessel, *The Duke of Montrose*.[2] This time he had been promoted to 2nd Officer.

34

We know that William visited Bath in March 1797, during the time he was still living at Racedown, visiting among other friends, the Speddings, mother and daughters, of Armathwaite Hall, Cumberland—then on a visit to Bath. William may have described this visit in a letter to John—and he would be anxious to see William and Dorothy, especially to visit them at Racedown. But by the end of June, early July, they had removed to Alfoxton Park, in the north of the county of Somerset, to be near Coleridge.

By a series of delays, John's ship had to put into Torbay, on the south Devon coast in July, and was kept there by adverse winds till September, eight weeks of enforced idleness. We know that William returned, from Alfoxton to Racedown to collect Peggy Marsh, Dorothy's faithful helper, and Basil, Montagu's little son, who was in their care, in August. With his brother and sister so near, as he thought, in Dorset only a few miles from Lyme, we can be sure that John would attempt to get to Racedown in the amount of leave he would have been granted during the eight weeks at Torbay.

Furthermore, to an experienced horseman like John, this distance would not be great. So that it is probable he met William in August 1797 when William returned to Racedown, as we have seen above. Whether they met earlier, during William's short visit to Bath, we can only conjecture.

But Jane Austen's description of Catherine Morland's introduction to Henry Tilney in the Lower Rooms at Bath has an echo of a personal encounter. Henry's knowledge of muslins is of particular interest here, when we remember that the Captains and officers of an East Indiaman were expected to do considerable trading on their own account, and bales of muslins from India would form a valuable part of the ship's return cargo. Henry Tilney's knowledge seems that of an experienced buyer of muslins. The conversation he has with Catherine's friend, Mrs. Allen, underlines this point:

' "This is a favourite gown, though it cost but nine shillings a yard."

' "That is exactly what I should have guessed it, Madam," said Mr. Tilney, looking at the muslin.

' "Do you understand muslins, Sir?"

' "Particularly well; I always buy my own cravats, and am allowed to be an excellent judge; and my sister has often trusted me in the choice of a gown. I bought one for her the other day, and it was pronounced to be a prodigious bargain by every lady who saw it. I gave but five shillings a yard for it, and a true Indian muslin."

'Mrs. Allen was quite struck by his genius. "Men commonly take so little notice of those things." said she. "I can never get Mr. Allen to know one of my gowns from another. You must be a great comfort to your sister, sir."

' "I hope I am, Madam." '

When his brother William married Mary Hutchinson, John gave her a new gown[3] to wear. Perhaps we can safely assume that the gown was made of Indian muslin, just as Henry Tilney's gift was to his sister. When John writes to Dorothy on October 22nd, 1802 he says, 'I am glad and rejoiced to hear that my sister Mary likes the choice of my new gown.'

It may also be remarked that Jane Austen is anxious to establish that it is perfectly 'respectable' for a gentleman to have a knowledge of trade. This may point to a desire on Jane's part to protect her 'nameless and dateless' lover from the snubs of some ill-mannered person, shown him because of his profession in the East India Company's Service, the Merchant Navy of the day, instead of being in 'the King's' service—as Mary Crawford calls the Navy when speaking of William Price to his sister in *Mansfield Park*. Even when speaking of the Navy, Mary Crawford disdains any rank below that of Admiral. Fanny's cousin, Edmund, says to Mary Crawford:

' "You have a large acquaintance in the Navy, I conclude?"

' "Among Admirals, large enough; but," with an air of grandeur, "we know very little of inferior ranks. Post-Captains may be a very good sort of men, but they do not belong to *us*. Of various Admirals I could tell you a great deal".'

It is perhaps more likely that Jane Austen and John Wordsworth first met at Lyme Regis. On his ride to and from Racedown, from Torbay, during the summer of 1797, he would find it a convenient resting point. Jane Austen's description of the little sea port, with its remarkably steep approaches, are vivid and personal. There is a quality of undeniable immediacy in the passage in *Persuasion* of the meeting with the unknown gentleman:

'When they came to the steps leading upwards from the beach, a gentleman at the same moment preparing to come down, politely drew back, and stopped to give them way. They ascended and passed him; and as they passed, Anne's face caught his eye, and he looked at her with a degree of earnest admiration, which she could not be insensible of. She was looking remarkably well; her very regular, very pretty features, having the bloom and freshness of youth restored by the fine wind which had been blowing on her complexion, and by the animation of eye which it had also produced. It was evident that the gentleman (completely a gentleman in manner) admired her exceedingly.'

Here the author is perhaps recalling the meeting (spoken of so many years later by Cassandra to a niece) during one of the summer and autumn rambles to the sea she made with her parents and sister, and perhaps Henry and their cousin, Eliza de Feuillide (whom he was to marry in December 1797) during the Steventon period.

As we have seen above, in July 1797, the Wordsworths had removed to Alfoxton, in the north of the county, from Racedown. This would make the description of Jane's 'nameless and dateless' lover (a visitor to the county, who had come there to see his brother) fit closely with that of John Wordsworth, the poet's sailor brother, also on shore, and also coming into the West Country to visit his brother. We know that William had a friend at Lyme named Leader, whom he sometimes visited during the Racedown period, and John may very well have called on this friend, interested as he too was in poetry. Or John may have had naval friends of his own at Lyme, as did Captain Wentworth.

The opening paragraph of Chapter 4 of *Persuasion* only requires a little adaptation as to names and date to make it fit fairly closely John's visit to his brother.

'He was not Mr. [Wordsworth], the former [tenant] of [Racedown], however suspicious appearances may be, but a Captain [John Wordsworth], his brother, who being made Commander [of an East Indiaman] . . . and not immediately employed, had come into Somersetshire, in the summer of [1797], and having no parent living, found a home for half a year at [his brother's house].'

We must, of course, allow Jane Austen to adapt, alter and disguise the facts to suit her purpose, recollected as these are many years later in tranquillity. In reality, John made his home for his long stay with his brother and sister later, in 1800, when they had moved up to Grasmere. During their sojourn in Somerset it is unlikely that John managed to pay them more than the very fleeting visit of August, when William returned to Racedown. But the date, 1797, coincides closely with the enforced idleness of John's ship, the Indiaman *Duke of Montrose* anchored in Torbay from July to September 22nd, and fits very well with the year of a possible ramble to the sea of the Austens, while they were still living at Steventon Rectory.

If the story of Jane's romance in the West Country is true

as regards the statement of Mrs. Bellas (her great niece), that 'this attachment must have been very deep', we can consider the description of Anne Elliot's attachment to Captain Wentworth, and his for her, as belonging to this time, and describing something very close to actuality. 'A short period of exquisite felicity followed, and but a short one . . .' Wentworth is described as 'a remarkably fine young man, with a great deal of intelligence, spirit and brilliancy'. John (Captain Wordsworth) is described in letters from William and Dorothy Wordsworth: 'he is grown "fat" and looked handsome—was in perfect health and excellent spirits.' 'He is grown a very tall, handsome man.' 'In the prime of health, a manly person; and one of the finest countenances ever seen.' William Wordsworth's description of his brother's character and qualities is worth quoting:

'He was . . . affectionate, silently enthusiastic, loving all quiet things, and a poet in everything but words.'

'He was modest and gentle . . . In everything his judgement was sound and original; his tastes in all the arts, music and poetry in particular, was exquisite; and his eye for the beauties of nature was as fine and delicate as ever poet or painter was gifted with; in some discriminations, owing to his education and way of life, far superior to any person I ever knew.'

When John Wordsworth came to Grasmere to his brother and sister, William and Dorothy, in January 1800 for a stay of nine months, we are safe in assuming that this was an unusual thing for him to do. It is true he was waiting to take command of his old ship, *The Earl of Abergavenny*, and therefore *had* to be on shore until the ship returned from her China voyage, but he usually divided his time among various members of the family and friends, and this long visit may have a deeper significance.

We do not know the names of any of John's own personal friends, nor where they lived, nor anything about them. But that he had friends who were interested in him, and in his career, is hinted at in some of his letters. One, to Dorothy, written from Forncett, where he is staying after leaving Grasmere, on his way down to London, is dated November 10th, 1800. He speaks of having visited his Cookson cousins, William and Christopher, away at school, twelve miles from Forncett, and is full of praise and admiration for the children.

He goes on to say, 'Norfolk at this time is looking naked and poor, and as I am no sportsman, it is a very uninteresting place to be at this time of the year.' He goes on to tell Dorothy of investments for his coming voyage. £2,000 from his cousin, Captain Wordsworth, £2,000 from Richard, and, '£1,500 from a quarter that I did not expect—none of our relations *or anybody that you are acquainted with.*'

Another letter, dated January 27th, 1801, to William this time, from London, speaks of the *Lyrical Ballads*—the second edition of which is coming out from Longman's the publisher, and John is supervising the despatch of letters and copies of the poems to various 'great men'. He also says, 'Some of my friends *that you are not acquainted with* have spoken in the most high terms of your poems.'

On February 16th, 1801, he writes to Mary Hutchinson and speaks of, '*Someone* has offered £5,000 investment for his voyage.'

He writes to Dorothy from Windsor on October 22nd, 1802—(having returned from his first voyage as Commander in August) where he has been visiting his Uncle Cookson. He tells Dorothy that he is going to Windsor again on the morrow—with his brother Richard (with whom he is staying at Staple Inn) riding there as they have horses, and going via Richmond and Hampton Court. He predicts a pleasant ride if the weather be fine.

Again on November 7th to Dorothy, he tells her: 'I have bought a horse and gig and drive all about London. *I can scarce tell you where I have been*; Windsor is nothing to me in distance. I am even going to see Christopher at Cambridge.' He speaks of being in very good health—for although he is living in London, he is getting 'all this country air' by means of his horse and gig.

So that it would seem that John had friends with whom his brother and sister were not acquainted at that time, and whom he visited when in the south. But for threequarters of a year, from January to the end of September, 1800, he preferred to be away from his friends, seeking instead the remote retreat of his brother and sister at Grasmere, a lonely quiet place.

We cannot know for certain why this was so, but we are free to guess John Wordsworth's reasons for wishing for a peaceful refuge away from everyone, and see if they fit the possible facts. He seems at this time to have a very pronounced feeling against 'grand' people—owners of large parks who may not allow a poor man to pasture his cows therein! This feeling goes on even after he has left his brother's home; in particular he inveighs against a neighbour of the Hutchinsons in Yorkshire—someone he calls 'Madame' Langley, who is a landowner of some importance, residing at Wykeham Abbey.

John writes to Mary Hutchinson, who is keeping house for her brother, the Langley's tenant farmer, Tom Hutchinson, at Gallow Hill, near Wykeham, on February 8th, 1801: 'As for her honour Madame Langley's improvements, what a pleasure I should take in finding fault with them. The Bridge would either be too large for the pond or too small or too high or too low and then the pond itself would be too large wasting too much good ground or miserably small and then for the plantation, for I suppose her honour cannot do without trees, it would be a vile and harsh system of firs and larches, chestnut, poplar, willows and laburnums. Now by the by how does her honour and his honour behave to you?—are they

like the lords and ladies I have seen, very proud, and pray—
have you got anybody that you can speak to?'

In this letter he is vigorously critical of 'Madame' Langley.
Perhaps it is because he is afraid she may be too proud and
haughty to be a good neighbour to the sister of one of Mr.
Langley's tenant farmers. John Wordsworth thus reveals his
state of mind, the irritability which caused him to seek out
the complete peace of his brother's lakeland home for a long
spell. He needed to be refreshed and soothed—he had been
hurt, his pride had been wounded, he was suffering from a
feeling of righteous anger. 'Madame' Langley may have reminded John Wordsworth of someone else, perhaps someone
who had hurt him deeply. How had this state of affairs come
about? We cannot believe that a handsome, original, talented
and interesting young man, such as we know John Wordsworth to have been, could have arrived at the age of twenty-
eight years without forming a romantic attachment. We do
not know the names of his friends—'not anybody that you
are acquainted with.'

May we turn to *Persuasion* and see if there is not a situation
to fit this state of mind, which we find John to be in in this
letter, which so sharply criticises 'Madame' Langley?

5. The Evidence——Emphasis on Persuasion

Captain Wentworth had no fortune . . .

JANE AUSTEN, *Persuasion*.

They tell me in eight or ten years I am to
be a very rich man.

JOHN WORDSWORTH.

'Captain Wentworth had no fortune. He had been lucky in
his profession, but spending freely, what had come freely, had
realised nothing. But, he was confident that he should soon
be rich; full of life and ardour, he knew that he should soon
have a ship, and soon be on a station that would lead to everything he wanted. He had always been lucky; he knew he
should be so still. Such confidence, powerful in its own
warmth, and bewitching in the wit which often expressed it,
must have been enough for Anne; but Lady Russell saw it
very differently. His sanguine temper, and fearlessness of
mind, operated very differently on her. She saw in it but an
aggravation of the evil. It only added a dangerous character
to himself. He was brilliant, he was headstrong.—Lady Russell
had little taste for wit; and of anything approaching to imprudence, a horror. She deprecated the connexion in every
light.

'Such opposition as these feelings produced, was more than
Anne could combat. Young and gentle as she was . . . Lady
Russell, whom she had always loved and relied on, could not,
with such steadiness of opinion, and such tenderness of

43

manner, be continually advising her in vain. She was persuaded to believe the engagement a wrong thing—indiscreet, improper, hardly capable of success, and not deserving it. But it was not a merely selfish caution, under which she acted, in putting an end to it. Had she not imagined herself consulting *his* good, even more than her own, she could hardly have given him up.—The belief of being prudent and self-denying principally for *his* advantage, was her chief consolation, under the misery of a parting—a final parting; and every consolation was required, for she had to encounter all the additional pain of opinions, on his side, totally unconvinced and unbending, and of his feeling himself ill-used by so forced a relinquishment. He left the country in consequence.'

Captain Wentworth felt himself ill-used. Lady Russell had come between him and his future bride. She had used her influence, the influence of an old friend to ruin his life. She had done it to protect her young friend, Anne Elliot, gentle creature that she was, from a life of poverty, in a cottage, with a nobody. That is how Lady Russell saw the situation. If we identify Anne with Jane herself, if we feel *Persuasion* is very largely autobiographical, we must then turn to Mrs. *Lefroy*, who stands in a like relationship to Jane Austen as Lady Russell does to Anne Elliot.

Mrs. Anne Lefroy was the daughter of Edward Brydges, of Wootton Court, Kent, and Jemima, his wife. *She* was the grand-daughter of Sir Francis Head. Mrs. Lefroy's husband, the Reverend Isaac Peter George Lefroy, was rector of Ashe, near Steventon, and her brother was Sir Samuel Egerton Brydges, the genealogist and antiquarian. He was an eccentric, and a snob, and sought to prove his family's connection with The Duke of Chandos. Anne Lefroy was a brilliant, attractive woman; being ten years younger than Mrs. Austen she became intimate with Jane, and when a young girl influenced and encouraged her considerably. But it is noticeable that she is

ambitious for Jane to make a suitable match. She did not
approve of Jane's friendship with Tom Lefroy, the Irish nephew, who stayed in Hampshire when Jane was twenty, in
1796. Tom was poor at that time, but was later to become
Chief Justice of Ireland.

'Mrs. Lefroy sent the gentleman off at the end of a very
few weeks, that no more mischief might be done.' Instead
she had been bringing forward the idea of a friend of hers as
a more suitably settled and well-connected husband for Jane.
There seems little doubt that he was a Mr. Blackall, of
Emmanuel College, Cambridge, later to become rector of North
Cadbury, in Somerset. But neither party to this suggestion
seemed enthusiastic; a meeting was not arranged and nothing
came of Mrs. Lefroy's match-making. Jane refers to the matter
in a letter to Cassandra, from Steventon to Godmersham :
'Mrs. Lefroy made no remarks on the letter [from Mr. Black-
all], nor did she indeed say anything about him as relative to
me. Perhaps she thinks she has said too much already . . .'

But that Mrs. Lefroy would have viewed John Wordsworth[1]
as an unsuitable suitor for Jane, we can be quite sure. She
would view the uncertainties of his career with grave disapproval, and his cheerful and happy confidence in his future
prospects would have been as likely to irritate her as Lady
Russell. In a letter to Mary Hutchinson, his future sister-in-
law, dated 5th December, 1800, from London, he says:
'Captain Wordsworth [his cousin and predecessor as Commander of *The Abergavenny*] has made a very handsome
fortune and is going to reside at Whitehaven; and they tell me
in 9 or 10 years I am to be a very rich man, for in that time
I am to make four voyages.'

That kind of optimism would have carried little weight with
Mrs. Lefroy, and Jane was no doubt influenced by her friend
against her own inner convictions, parting most miserably
from John Wordsworth, after a 'short period of exquisite

felicity . . .' That Jane Austen bitterly regretted her friend's
advice is very likely. Had she consulted only her own feelings,
or those of her parents, whose own 'early warm attachment'
(and early adventurous marriage) was a shining example of a
'cheerful confidence in futurity, against that over anxious
caution which seems to insult exertion and distrust
Providence!'—had she trusted to these wiser counsels, all
would have been well.

We can imagine the angry, hurt feelings with which John
Wordsworth[2] left Jane; he knew his dismissal had all been
Mrs. Lefroy's doing (was he responsible for the title 'Madame'
Lefroy—as he was later to call Mrs. Langley?) he knew that
he and Jane were ideally suited to each other—in similarity
of family background, in temperament, in tastes of all kinds.
He knew they would neither find anyone else to whom they
could be equally devoted. But pride, bitter and agonising,
made the shy, sensitive sailor determine to try, as best he
could, to forget his deep love for Jane.

And so, when the opportunity came for a long holiday, he
took the seemingly wise step of going into a 'country' which
had no connection with his lost love—his beloved lakeland.
So it was that his sojourn with William and Dorothy at Grasmere in 1800, and his friendship with the Hutchinson sisters,
may be thought of as a similar situation to the one described
by Jane Austen in *Persuasion*. The Musgrove sisters were to
have driven Anne Elliot from Captain Wentworth's heart.
But instead, Louisa, the one thought of as being attached to
Captain Wentworth, marries Captain Benwick, a brother
officer. In real life, one of the Hutchinson sisters, Mary, marries William Wordsworth, John's brother. But through John's
friendship with this gentle, sweet woman, it is possible to see
a healing process gradually emerging. We are told John
accompanied Mary 'everywhere' during her six weeks' visit to
Grasmere in the spring of 1800.

The Evidence—Emphasis on Persuasion

It can be safely assumed that out of the four Wordsworth brothers William and John were closest to one another. They had more in common—although at his first coming to stay at Grasmere in January 1800, William felt he was almost a stranger, the old bond soon returned. William describes his feelings in the 'Silver-How Poem':

'When thou hadst quitted Esthwaite's
pleasant shore,
And taken thy first leave of those green hills
And rocks that were the play-ground of thy youth,
Year followed year, my Brother! and we two,
Conversing not, knew little in what mould
Each other's mind was fashioned; and at length,
When once again we met in Grasmere Vale,
Between us there was little other bond
Than common feelings of fraternal love.
But thou, a schoolboy, to the sea hadst carried
Undying recollections; Nature there
Was with thee; She, who loved us both she still
Was with thee; and even so didst thou become
A *silent* poet; from the solitude
Of the vast sea didst bring a watchful heart
Still couchant, an inevitable ear,
And an eye practised like a blind man's touch.
—Back to the joyless ocean thou art gone;
Nor from this vestige of the musing hours
Could I withhold thy honoured name—and now
I love the fir-grove with a perfect love.
Thither do I withdraw when cloudless suns
Shine hot, or wind blows troublesome and strong;
And there I sit at evening, when the steep
Of Silver-How, and Grasmere's peaceful lake
And one green island, gleam between the stems

Of the dark firs, a visionary scene!
And while I gaze upon the spectacle
O clouded splendour, on this dream-like sight
Of solemn loveliness, I think on thee,
My Brother, and on all which thou hast lost.
Nor seldom, if I rightly guess, while thou,
Muttering the verses which I muttered first
Among the mountains, through the midnight watch
Art pacing thoughtfully the vessel's deck
In some far region, here, while o'er my head,
At every impulse of the moving breeze,
The fir-grove murmurs with a sea-like sound,
Alone I tread this path;—for aught I know,
Timing my steps to thine; and with a store
Of undistinguishable sympathies.'

This closeness between these two brothers, William and
John, this store of 'undistinguishable sympathies', is perhaps
only gradually becoming recognised as we come to know more
about John. Having this intimate brotherly love, they were
able to understand and sympathise with the personal feelings
and difficulties of the other.

We must believe it would be likely that John would have
known about Annette long before the sojourn in Grasmere of
1800—he was probably told when William came back to England, to London, in December 1792, and stayed with Richard
in Staple Inn. John may have been able to meet him, in between voyages, perhaps in London or Southampton, or the
Isle of Wight, to comfort and advise William about the
practicability of a return to France, the possibility of a boat.
We know William went down to Gravesend to meet John for
his Christmas holidays in 1789 from Cambridge, and he may
have done so on a later occasion. Being out of favour with his
older relatives because of his sympathy with the French, and

because of the Annette affair, would incline William to draw closer to the sympathetic John whenever he was in England at this difficult period. But these meetings were only glimpses; the long stay of 1800 at Grasmere confirmed their devotion and tender understanding of each other.

John may very well have unburdened himself to William about his unsuccessful love for Jane Austen. William, sympathetic and full of 'a tenderness that never sleeps' as only a man who had himself suffered, could understand and sympathise, advised John to talk to Mary about it when opportunity offered. William felt sure that she would counsel him aright; she, with her calm, sweet and wise nature, would know what could be done, what course he should take. To an outsider, an onlooker, it may well have seemed that there was a deeper friendship growing, but William knew it was not so and that John and Mary were friendly as a brother and sister are, and should be, friends.[3]

Tom Hutchinson and his sister Mary became neighbours of Francis Wrangham, William's college friend, when he was inducted to the rectory of Hunmanby, Yorkshire, early in 1796. William in a letter of February, 1801, to Wrangham shows his deep concern for Mary; for her possible loneliness at Gallow Hill, her brother's farm:

'I need not say how much I was disappointed in not seeing you at your parsonage house. Though I was much pressed for time I purposed to stop at least a couple of days with you. I called in company with a Mr. Hutchinson who lives at Gallow Hill, near Wykeham. He is one of Mr. Langley's Farmers, and a particular friend of mine. At the time when we called at Hunmanby, my brother John and I were staying in Mr. Hutchinson's house, a visit which we prolonged for three weeks. Mr. Hutchinson's house is kept by his sister, a woman who is a very particular friend of both my sister and myself. If ever you go that way it would be a great kindness done to me if you would call on them, and also at any future period render them any service in your power: I mean as to lending Miss Hutchinson books, or when you become acquainted with them, performing them any little service, aupres de Monsieur ou Madame Langley, with respect to their farm. Miss Hutchinson I can recommend to you as a most amiable and good creature, with whom you would converse with great pleasure.'

William's growing awareness of his closeness to Mary and his need of her, from her visit to Racedown in 1797 to his frequent visits to her, and hers to him, from 1799 to 1802, must have made him acknowledge in his heart of hearts that she was the one chosen to be his wife; no straining after anyone, or actively going in search of a wife among strangers, but a natural process, calm and sure.[4] These feelings William must have spoken of to John, and although William was not formally engaged to Mary at the time of John's long sojourn with them, it seems most likely that the brothers shared the knowledge of the situation as regards William's hope of marriage to Mary as soon as a meeting with Annette was once again possible.

It would have been at this time, 1800, that Mary suggested to John Wordsworth that he should send, through William's publishers, Longman's, the new edition of the poems to Jane, when they came out. This he would have done in January 1801, when he was in London, waiting to take command of his ship, *The Earl of Abergavenny* and seeing the poems sent off to various people on William's behalf. Among criticisms of the poems, in a letter to Coleridge dated April 1801, William quotes John as saying:

'To a lady, a friend of mine, I gave the 2 vol: they were both new to her. "The Idiot Boy" of all the poems her delight; could talk of nothing else.'

Being able to correspond with Jane Austen, on the subject of William's poems, as Mary had suggested, was a wonderful way of renewing their friendship, and opened up a possible healing of the sad rift occasioned by Mrs. Lefroy's interference. In this connection it is fascinating to remember that Jane's brother, George, about whom we hear so little, was most possibly an 'idiot'—or was 'mentally retarded' as we would say in our modern jargon. We do not know; but we can be sure that she had a most tender feeling for her unfortunate brother George, and may have shared William's views on the subject of the care of idiot children.

There is a letter of his to John Wilson, of June 1802, where William states these views: 'the loathing and disgust which many people have at the sight of an idiot, is a feeling which, though having some foundation in human nature, is not necessarily attached to it in any virtuous degree, but is owing in great measure to a false delicacy, and, if I may say it without rudeness, a certain want of comprehensiveness of thinking and feeling. Persons in the lower classes of society have little or nothing of this: if an idiot is born in a poor man's house, it must be taken care of, and cannot be boarded out, as it would be by gentlefolks, or sent to a public or private asylum for such unfortunate beings. Poor people, seeing frequently among their neighbours such objects, easily forget whatever there is of natural disgust about them, and have therefore a sane state, so that without pain or suffering they perform their duties towards them . . . I have often applied to idiots, in my own mind, that sublime expression of Scripture, that "their life is hidden with God." They are worshipped, probably from a feeling of this sort, in several parts of the East . . . I have indeed often looked upon the conduct of fathers and mothers of the lower classes of society towards idiots as the great triumph of the human heart. It is there that we see the strength, disinterestedness, and grandeur of love; nor have I ever been able to contemplate an object that calls out so many excellent and virtuous sentiments without finding it hallowed thereby, and having something in me which bears down before it, like a deluge, every feeble sensation of disgust and aversion.'

In a letter dated 27th December, 1808, from Southampton, Jane Austen writing to Cassandra, speaks of meeting a Mr. Fitzhugh, who was totally deaf. She says: 'I talked to him a little with my fingers . . .'

Years before, in 1770, Mrs. Austen had written to Mrs. Walter and speaks of her son George, then aged four years: 'My poor little George is come to see me to-day, he seems pretty well, though he had a fit lately; it was a twelvemonth since he had one before, so was in hopes they had left him, but must not flatter myself so now.' Chapman in *Facts and Problems* says of George, the second son: 'If he never learned to talk, might that explain Jane's knowledge of the dumb alphabet?' It seems likely that she would visit her brother, and communicated with him in that way. It would also have given her that warm appreciation of *The Idiot Boy* and partly explain her enthusiasm for it. But the spontaneous wit of the poem and its clever shapeliness would also appeal to her.

Through the renewal of a correspondence in the early spring of 1801, on the subject of William's poetry, John Wordsworth and Jane Austen would gradually become acquainted again. There would have been the long gap of John's voyage—from May 1801 to August 1802, when it is unlikely that they corresponded. Jane would have waited and hoped for a resumption of their friendship in the autumn of 1802.

That summer she had accompanied her parents and Cassandra to Dawlish[5] and Teignmouth; Jane and Cassandra then went on to stay at Steventon with the James Austens, Jane perhaps hoping John might visit her there? She would know he had landed again from the navy lists and newspapers. She and Cassandra then went on to stay at Godmersham, with the Edward Austens. By the end of October they were back at

Steventon, and after a stay of about three weeks they went on to Manydown, to visit their friends the Bigg Withers.

It was during this visit, after they had been there about a week, that a most curious incident took place, an occurrence quite out of character with Jane's usual considerate behaviour to her family and friends. Her stay at Manydown was cut short; the sisters returned to Steventon, and begged James to escort them back to their parents at Bath—at great inconvenience to James, as being a weekend (December 3rd, 1802) he had not time to provide a substitute for the Steventon church services on the Sunday.

It appears that Harris Bigg Wither proposed marriage to Jane and she accepted him. But the next day, or sooner, she regretted her decision and told him she could not marry him. So the decision to leave Manydown and to return home immediately was made. Why was this? What had caused this strange change of mind in this normally gentle and rational creature?

The bare facts of the date of the autumn visits of Cassandra and Jane in 1802 convey a certain 'restlessness'—as though Jane, accompanied by the ever faithful Cassandra, is darting about, unsettled, uncertain, unhappy; 'never so weary, never so in woe.'

Let us look at these bare facts, set out in Mrs. James Austen's Diary. On September 1st Cassandra and Jane arrive at Steventon Rectory, their old home, and now the home of James and Mary Austen and their children. On September 3rd they leave for Edward Austen's home at Godmersham, Kent; October 28th they return to Steventon; 25th November they leave for Manydown; 3rd December they return to Steventon; 4th December they return to Bath.

Could it be that Jane was anxious to be in a place where John Wordsworth could easily find her? Did she feel that Bath was too far away? We are told that Jane fainted when the decision to leave Steventon and live in Bath was first announced; and John would know nothing of their removal to Bath.

Perhaps someone—probably her close friend Anne Sharpe —sent Jane a copy of the newspaper, the *York Herald* of October 9th, 1802. The entry of William Wordsworth's marriage to Mary Hutchinson may have increased Jane's distress:

'On Monday last was married at Brompton, Mr. Wordsworth of Grasmere to Miss Hutchinson of Gallow Hill, near Scarboro'.'

This short notice may have convinced Jane that John *had* forgotten her, and married one of the Hutchinson girls. There were no initials given, and Mr. Wordsworth could be either William or John.

6. *More Evidence in the Novels*

If then true lovers have been ever cross'd,
It stands as an edict in destiny:
Then let us teach our trial patience,
Because it is a customary cross,
As due to love, as thoughts, and dreams, and
    sighs,
Wishes and tears . . .

WILLIAM SHAKESPEARE,
A *Midsummer Night's Dream*, Act I, Sc. I.

Lovers at cross-purposes, wandering in a wood, missing one another, as in a Shakespeare play, mistaken identity—these themes occur more than once in the novels of Jane Austen. It is as though the characters are moving about blindly, veiled in a thick fog, unable to penetrate, to reach out to one another. This mist in which they are travelling, groping, is in reality their own pride, resentment, folly. Till they have shed these shackles, these burdens, they cannot step out into the clarity and beauty of the day. Being the great creative artist and thinker that she is, Jane Austen knows that real life is like that too.

This sense of frustration, of missing one another, occurs in *Pride and Prejudice*, when Jane Bennet, in London on a visit to her Uncle and Aunt Gardiner, does not meet Charles Bingley as she had hoped, and is made unhappy by his apparent neglect. In fact he had been told Jane no longer loved him; his family and his friend do not think the connection 'good enough' for him, and keep him misinformed. Charles Bingley is perhaps suggested by Charles Lloyd, of Bingley

Hall, Birmingham, a friend and relative by marriage of the Wordsworths.

In *Northanger Abbey* this feeling of frustration, of loving feelings thwarted by selfishness, of lovers at cross-purposes is underlined when Catherine Morland, having promised to take a country walk with Eleanor and her brother, Henry Tilney, is tricked into going for a drive with the overbearing John Thorpe, who again tells an untruth to get his own way, and Catherine is prevented from meeting the man she loves.

In *Sense and Sensibility* the frustration and separation are keenly felt. In the London sojourn of Elinor and Marianne Dashwood, when Marianne hopes Willoughby will visit her at Mrs. Jennings' house where they are staying, he does not call. Instead Marianne hears of his engagement to a wealthy heiress. She sees him at a party, but he does not come to her willingly, and his indifference is an agonising awakening for her.

In *Mansfield Park*, the heroine Fanny Price, as she gradually grows aware of her love for her cousin, Edmund Bertram, is kept apart from him for almost the whole book by his blind attachment to an unscrupulous woman. The theme of the star-cross'd lovers is symbolised in their wanderings in the wood at Sotherton—and the irritation and exhaustion felt by the pairs of lovers . . .

> 'Never so weary, never so in woe,
> Bedabbled with dew, torn with briars,
> I can no further crawl, no further go;
> My legs can keep no pace with my desires.'

In *Emma* the theme of frustration, of cross-purposes and wandering in a wood, is maintained in both the main plot and the sub-plot of Jane Fairfax's secret. Emma is blissfully protected from its sorrows through her own vanity, her own blindness, till repentance, full acceptance and humility lead her at last to Mr. Knightley. But it is in Jane Fairfax's secret love of Frank Churchill that we are coming closer to Jane Austen's own story of wandering, frustration and cross-purposes, in her search for the lover she had rejected, under pressure, years ago.

In the letter John Wordsworth wrote to his sister on November 7th, 1802 from London (quoted above) he tells her that he had been to the play, Mr. Reynolds' new comedy of *Delays and Blunders*, first produced on October 31st of that year at The Theatre Royal, Covent Garden. He also saw *Richard III* 'but it is no more like Shakespeare has written than Jack the Giant killer!' It is worth noticing that Reynolds' play *The Dramatist*, produced in 1789, was considered one of the most original of the eighteenth century comedies, and 'makes ample atonement for the pitiful farces and murderous Shakespearean adaptations of which Reynolds[1] was guilty in his after years.' If the adaptation of *Richard III* which John saw was also by Reynolds, his condemnation is excusable! He would have gone to see the new comedy some time between meeting William and Dorothy on their return from France in September 1802, and writing his letter.

Jane Austen, as we have seen, was at Godmersham from September 3rd till October 28th. It would have been a possibility for her to have gone on to London after leaving Godmersham, staying with Henry and Eliza, then living possibly still at 24 Upper Berkeley Street, but there are no letters to record the visit. It is most probable that Henry would escort his sisters on their way through London, from Godmersham to Steventon, to continue their visit to James and Mary Austen at the Rectory. But they would almost certainly spend a few days with Henry and Eliza beforehand, and they may have been to the theatre at this time. Like John, Jane was a keen theatre goer, and she may very well have been at the first night of Reynolds' play *Delays and Blunders*. It is worth while here to notice the use of the word 'Blunder', (in *Emma*) spelt out by Frank Churchill, using the Knightley children's alphabet letters, and pushed by him towards Jane Fairfax, after his unwitting disclosure about the Perry's intention to keep a carriage—a secret which he could only have known through Jane's letter to him.

In Reynolds' play *The Dramatist*, there is a strange similarity to a scene in *Emma*—which has a personal feel about it. This scene, which Jane may possibly have discussed with John, is the first of the play:

'Act I. Scene I. The Grove.—Lady Waitfort's House, Bath. A window open, and music is heard.

'*Letty*. "Pray, has she taught you why she never plays any tune but the one we heard just now?"

'*Marianne*. "Yes—and if you'll keep it a secret, I'll tell you, Letty,—Mr. Harry Neville taught it her last summer,—and now she is always playing it because it puts her in mind of the dear man,—when it is ended, don't you observe how she sighs from the bottom of her dear little heart?"'

In *Emma*, Chapter 28, Mrs. Weston and Emma call at Mrs. Bates' home, where Frank Churchill, Jane Fairfax and Mrs. and Miss Bates are all collected; Jane is trying out her new pianoforte. A window is opened by Miss Bates, her aunt, to speak to Mr. Knightley as he passes on horseback in the street below. Just before Miss Bates' conversation with Knightley, Frank Churchill and Emma are discussing the new instrument sent to Jane; they conjecture it was sent by her friend and guardian, Colonel Campbell. Frank asks Jane to play something. Then follows a request of Frank's which bears the ring of a recollected happening. '"If you are very kind," said he, "it will be one of the waltzes we danced last night;—let me live them over again . . . I would have given worlds—all the worlds one ever has to give—for another half hour . . ."

'She played. "What felicity it is to hear a tune again

58

which *has* made one happy!—If I mistake not that was danced at Weymouth."

'She looked up at him for a moment, coloured deeply, and played something else . . .'

Frank Churchill then returns to Emma, and continues his conversation with her about Jane and her new instrument. ' "And here are a new set of Irish melodies . . . This was all sent with the instrument . . . He knew Miss Fairfax could have no music here. I honour that part of the attention particularly; it shows it to have been so thoroughly from the heart. Nothing hastily done . . . True affection only could have prompted it."

'Emma could not help being amused; and when on glancing her eye towards Jane Fairfax she caught the remains of a smile, when she saw that with all the blush of consciousness, there had been a smile of secret delight . . . she had . . . much less compunction with respect to her. This amiable, upright, perfect Jane Fairfax was apparently cherishing very reprehensible feelings.

' ". . . She is playing Robin Adair at this moment—*his* favourite." '

The contrast of the happiness (even though for the time being it is marred by the need for secrecy) of this love and engagement between Frank Churchill and Jane Fairfax, and the anguished searches of both Jane Bennet and Marianne Dashwood, during their visits to London, seem to underline the poignancy of the following scene of a possible meeting between Jane Austen and John Wordsworth in the autumn of 1802.

If we can allow ourselves to imagine the scene—at the theatre, perhaps Covent Garden. Jane is with her sister Cassandra and Henry and Eliza, also George and Mary Cooke, her cousins, of Great Bookham—and perhaps some of the Godmersham family in the party. Jane has not heard again from John Wordsworth since his landing in August 1802. She has been in a state of nervous tension and anxiety—quite unlike herself—wondering if she will see him during this short visit to London, which had been planned to take place from Godmersham at the end of the autumn visit to Edward and his family.

Then Jane reads of John's marriage, as she mistakenly thinks, in the Yorkshire newspaper of October 9th. Across the theatre, as the lights are lit she recognises him, a tall, handsome man, little changed by the four years of their estrangement. He is with a party too—Captain and Mrs. Wordsworth, or the Robinsons, and other friends. Jane does not know them, and thinks one of the ladies must be his newly-married wife. He in his turn is shy and proud—she seems remote amidst her party of companions, and he does not feel she wishes to acknowledge him. George Cooke, her cousin, is young and handsome, and attentive to her. John Wordsworth cannot know why Jane has turned away with only a faint acknowledgement. He could not realise that she mistakenly identified the bridegroom in the notice of William's marriage to Mary as himself. It is interesting to notice here the mistaken identity of the brothers Edward and Robert Ferrars in *Sense and Sensibility*—and Elinor's joy when she discovers Edward to be free!

In his letter of November 7th to Dorothy, John had said: 'It is not quite so bad as I thought it would have been from what you said.' He is referring to the announcement of William's marriage in the London paper of October 9th,—the *Morning Post*. This notice annoyed the Wordsworths—they did not care to be advertised as though they were part of the attractions of a tourist resort. It was thought to have been a joke—sent in possibly by Charles Lamb or Coleridge. It ran thus:

'Monday last, W. Wordsworth, Esq. was married to Miss

Hutchinson, of Wykeham, near Scarborough, and proceeded immediately, with his wife and his sister, for his charming cottage in the little Paradise Vale of Grasmere . . .'

When Jane Austen rejected Harris Bigg Wither, of Manydown Park, Hampshire, and asked to be taken back to Bath, she realised that she had been wrong, very wrong, in accepting his offer of marriage, at first. She realised that, for her, a marriage to a respectably situated landowning neighbour's son—without real affection, without love—could never for her constitute a marriage at all. So she returned to her father's house at Bath. This realisation would have been quite enough of a reason for her to reject Harris. No more striking reason need be expected.

Yet there may have been a further reason—clear and definite. We know that she had most possibly seen the notice of William's marriage ('Mr. Wordsworth') in the York newspaper. But we do *not* know when she saw the more elaborate and informative notice in the *Morning Post*. If we suppose Jane did not read this notice until she reached Manydown—'perhaps chancing upon a pile of these newspapers in the library at her friends' house—where she had retired for peace and reflection—after accepting Harris Bigg Wither's proposal. Among the back copies she would find the one for October 9th, and read the notice of the marriage—and realise at last that the bridegroom had been, not John, but William!

If we think of Anne Elliot's feelings after reading Mary Musgrove's letter telling her that Louisa is to marry not Captain Wentworth but Captain Benwick, perhaps we shall be very near to knowing what Jane's feelings were like at that moment.

'Mary need not have feared her sister's being in any degree prepared for the news. She had never in her life been more astonished. Captain Benwick and Louisa Musgrove! It was almost too wonderful for belief . . . The conclusion of the whole was, that if the woman who had been sensible of Captain Wentworth's merits could be allowed to prefer another man, there was nothing in the engagement to excite lasting wonder; and if Captain Wentworth lost no friend by it, certainly nothing to be regretted. No, it was not regret which made Anne's heart beat in spite of herself, and brought the colour into her cheeks when she thought of Captain Wentworth unshackled and free. She had some feelings which she was ashamed to investigate. They were too much like joy, senseless[2] joy!'

While Jane returns unexpectedly to her parents' house at 4 Sydney Place, Bath, John Wordsworth is still in London. He writes to his sister Dorothy on December 1st and again on December 17th, having recently returned from a stay with his uncle, Canon Cookson, and his wife Dorothy Cookson, and their children, then in residence at Windsor.

His chance meeting with Jane at the play towards the end of October, and the attentive young man in her party (in reality her cousin, George Cooke), make John decide to find out once and for all if she still has any regard for him. Having heard of Mr. Austen's removal from Steventon Rectory, and his now being settled at Bath, John sets out from Windsor, travelling to Bath in his own gig. Perhaps there is something of the agony of mind of Willoughby's lonely ride, when he is riding towards (as he thinks) the dying Marianne; it may be appropriate in this context, remembering Jane's face of utter misery at their original parting, and broken engagement. 'I had seen Marianne's sweet face as white as death . . . she was before me, constantly before me, as I travelled, in the same look and hue.'

Once in Bath it is an easy matter to discover the Austens' address. But a much more difficult matter, to a man as shy and diffident as John Wordsworth to screw up his courage and boldly call up them. Instead, he lingers away his time,

hoping to meet with them at a public gathering—at the
Rooms, or out walking. He had determined on staying only a
week in Bath, and if he had not the luck to meet Jane by the
end of that time, he resolved to quit the town, and give up
all hope of seeing her. But he was lucky—he catches sight of
her at the Rooms in the evening . . .

'Captain Wentworth walked in alone. Anne was nearest
to him, and making yet a little advance, she instantly spoke.
He was preparing only to bow and pass on, but her gentle
"How do you do?" brought him out of the straight line to
stand near her, and make enquiries in return,' and to speak to
her alone for some time. And then later that same evening
in the concert room, Captain Wentworth becomes separated
from Anne . . .

'On stepping back from the group, to be joined again by
Captain Wentworth, she saw that he was gone. She was just
in time to see him turn into the concert room. He was gone—
he had disappeared: she felt a moment's regret. But they
should meet again. He would look for her—he would find her
out long before the evening were over—and at present, perhaps, it was as well to be asunder. She was in need of a little
interval for reflection . . .

'. . . Anne saw nothing, thought nothing of the brilliancy
of the room. Her happiness was from within. Her eyes were
bright, and her cheeks glowed, but she knew nothing about
it. She was thinking only of the last half hour, and as they
passed to their seats, her mind took a hasty range over it. His
choice of subjects, his expressions, and still more his manner
and look, had been such as she could see in only one light.
His opinion of Louisa Musgrove's inferiority, an opinion
which he had seemed solicitous to give, his wonder at Captain
Benwick, his feelings as to a first, strong attachment—
sentences begun which he could not finish—his half averted
eyes, and more than half expressive glance, all, all declared

that he had a heart returning to her at least; that anger, resentment, avoidance, were no more; and that they were succeeded, not merely by friendship and regard, but by the tenderness of the past; yes, some share of the tenderness of the past. She could not contemplate the change as implying less. He must love her.'

But John Wordsworth—like his counterpart in the novel—feels himself to be less fortunate in the circumstances of Jane being too much engaged with others of her party—especially with the same young man he had observed with her in London. But Jane is, like Anne Elliot at the concert, anxious for another opportunity of speaking to John.

'Anne's eyes had caught the right direction, and distinguished Captain Wentworth, standing among a cluster of men at a little distance. As her eyes fell on him, his seemed to be withdrawn from her. It had that appearance. It seemed as if she had been one moment too late; and as long as she dared to observe, he did not look again : but the performance was re-commencing, and she was forced to seem to restore her attention to the orchestra, and look straight forward.

'When she could give another glance, he had moved away. He could not have come nearer to her if he would; she was so surrounded and shut in : but she would rather have caught his eye.

'Mr. Elliot's speech too distressed her. She had no longer any inclination to talk to him. She wished him not so near. The first act was over. Now she hoped for some beneficial change; and, after a period of nothing-saying amongst the party, some of them did decide on going in quest of tea. Anne was one of the few who did not choose to move. She remained in her seat, and so did Lady Russell; but she had the pleasure of getting rid of Mr. Elliot; and she did not mean, whatever she might feel on Lady Russell's account, to shrink from conversation with Captain Wentworth if he gave her the opportunity . . . He did not come however. Anne fancied she discerned him at a distance, but he never came. The anxious interval wore away unproductively. The others returned, the room filled again, benches were reclaimed and re-possessed, and another hour of music was to give delight or the gapes, as real or affected taste for it prevailed. To Anne, it chiefly wore the prospect of an hour of agitation. She could not quit that room in peace without seeing Captain Wentworth once more, without the interchange of one friendly look.

In re-settling themselves, there were now many changes, the result of which were favourable for her . . . Mr. Elliot was invited by Elizabeth and Miss Carteret, in a manner not to be refused, to sit between them; and by some other removals, and a little scheming of her own, Anne was enabled to place herself much nearer the end of the bench than she had been before, much more within reach of a passer-by . . .

'Such was her situation, with a vacant space at hand, when Captain Wentworth was again in sight. She saw him not far off. He saw her too; yet he looked grave, and seemed irresolute, and only by very slow degrees came at last near enough to speak to her. She felt that something must be the matter. The change was indubitable. The difference between his present air and what it had been in the Octagon Room was strikingly great. Why was it? She thought of her father—of Lady Russell. Could there have been any unpleasant glances? He began by speaking of the concert, gravely; more like the Captain Wentworth of Uppercross; owned himself disappointed, had expected better singing; and in short, must confess that he should not be sorry when it was over. Anne replied, and spoke in defence of the performance so well, and yet in allowance for his feelings, so pleasantly, that his countenance improved, and he replied again with almost a smile. They talked for a few minutes more; the improvement held; he even looked down towards the bench, as if he saw a place on it well worth occupying; when, at that moment, a touch on her shoulder obliged Anne to turn round. It came from Mr. Elliot. He begged her pardon, but she must be applied to, to explain Italian again. Miss Carteret was very anxious to have a general idea of what was next to be sung. Anne could not refuse; but never had she sacrificed to politeness with a more suffering spirit.

'A few minutes, though as few as possible, were inevitably consumed; and when her own mistress again, when able to turn and look as she had done before, she found herself accosted by Captain Wentworth, in a reserved yet hurried sort of farewell. "He must wish her good-night. He was going —he should get home as fast as he could."

' "Is not this song worth staying for?" said Anne, suddenly struck by an idea which made her yet more anxious to be encouraging.

' "No!" he replied impressively, "there is nothing worth my staying for;" and he was gone directly.

'Jealousy of Mr. Elliot! It was the only intelligible motive. Captain Wentworth jealous of her affection! Could she have believed it a week ago—three hours ago! For a moment the gratification was exquisite. But alas! there were very different thoughts to succeed. How was such jealousy to be quieted? How was the truth to reach him? How, in all the peculiar disadvantages of their respective situations, would he ever learn her real sentiments? It was misery to think of Mr. Elliot's attentions. Their evil was incalculable.'

So John Wordsworth left the concert, undecided as to Jane's attitude towards him. No one can read this scene from *Persuasion*—of the meeting of Anne at the concert in Bath, and not be aware of a compelling autobiographical 'ring of truth' about it all. The 'actors' in the real life scene would be just as likely to cause John the same jealous misgivings. There would possibly have been Jane's uncle and aunt—Mr. and

Mrs. James Leigh-Perrot, a Mrs. Welby, Mrs. Leigh-Perrot's niece, a daughter of the Governor of Barbados—a fashionable young woman, who sang duets with the Prince Regent; George and Mary Cooke, Jane's cousins—George being attentive and kind to Jane, may have caused John's jealousy and hasty departure; and possibly too the Henry Austens would be among the party.

On his last day before his return to London, John finally resolves to call at Sydney Place; it would have taken all his desperate resolution and courage to come to such a decision. But his courage and resolution were not after all put to the test, for providence in this instance dealt more gently with him. We may imagine that his cousin, Captain Wordsworth, who was staying in Bath with his wife ('they were both much delighted with Bath, and think no place like it')[3] meets Jane as she is walking home, the day after the concert, 'and within a few steps of his own door'. Possibly they had been acquainted with the Austens since they had settled in Bath.

Captain Wordsworth would have persuaded Jane into their house to call for a moment on his wife, a charming lady, who may have taken a great fancy to Jane at an earlier meeting. As they ascend to the drawing room, Captain Wordsworth tells Jane that they are all alone—'only John is with us'. She is horrified, and has no time to decide how to extricate herself and rush away, before she is ushered into the room while the Captain goes off in search of his wife. Jane thinks the room is empty at first, then observes John, reading by the fire. He is as astonished and embarrassed as she is! They gradually become more at ease—and by the time Mrs. Wordsworth comes to greet Jane, they have been able to go through a good part of the causes of John's jealousy and determination to return to London after one more day. He learns that Jane is *not* in love with her cousin, George Cooke—and there is no truth in any rumour of her attachment to anyone . . . In the cancelled chapter of *Persuasion* will be found a most moving and most authentic account of their reconciliation.

' "You are misin—the Admiral is misinformed. I do justice to the kindness of his intentions, but he is quite mistaken. There is no truth in any such report."

'He was a moment silent. She turned her eyes towards him for the first time since his re-entering the room. His colour was varying, and he was looking at her with all the power and keenness which she believed no other[4] eyes, than his possessed.

' "No truth in any such report?" he repeated. "No truth in any part of it?" "None".

'He had been standing by a chair, enjoying the relief of leaning on it, or of[5] playing with it. He now sat down, drew it a little nearer to her, and looked with an expression which had something more than penetration in it—something softer. Her countenance did not discourage. It was a silent but a very powerful dialogue; on his side supplication, on hers acceptance. Still a little nearer, and a hand taken and pressed; and "Anne, my own dear Anne!" bursting forth in the fulness of ex-quisite feeling, and all suspense and indecision were over. They were re-united. They were carried back to the past with only an increase of attachment and confidence, and only such a flutter of present delight as made them little fit for the interruption of Mrs. Croft when she joined them not long afterwards. She probably, in the observations of the next ten minutes saw something to suspect; and though it was hardly possible for a woman of her description to wish the mantua-maker had imprisoned her longer, she might be very likely wishing for some excuse to run about the house, some storm to break the window above, or a summons to the Admiral's shoemaker below.

'Fortune favoured them all, however, in another way, in a gentle steady rain, just happily set in as the Admiral returned and Anne rose to go. She was earnestly invited to stay dinner. A note was despatched to Camden Place, and she staid —staid till ten at night; during that time the husband and wife, either by the wife's contrivance, or by simply going on in their usual way, were frequently out of the room together— gone upstairs to hear a noise, or downstairs to settle their accounts, or upon the landing place to trim the lamp. And these precious moments were turned to so good an account that all the most anxious feelings of the past were gone through. Before they parted at night, Anne had the felicity of being assured that in the first place (so far from being altered for the worse), she had gained expressibly in personal loveliness; and as to character, hers was now fixed on his mind as perfection itself, maintaining the just medium of fortitude and gentleness—that he had never ceased to love and prefer her, though it had only been at Uppercross that he had learnt to do her justice, and only at Lyme he had received lessons of more than one kind . . . he had seen everything to exalt in his estimation the woman he had lost, and there begun to deplore the pride, the folly, the madness of resentment, which had kept him from trying to regain her when thrown in his way. From that period to the present had his penance been the most severe . . . He had remained in Shropshire lamenting the blindness of his own calculations, till at once released from Louisa by the astonishing felicity of her engagement to Benwick.

'Bath—Bath had instantly followed in thought and not long after in fact. To Bath—to arrive with hope, to be torn by jealousy at the first sight of Mr. Elliot; to experience all the changes of each concert; to be miserable by this morning's circumstantial report, to be now more happy than language could express, or any heart but his own be capable of.

'He was very eager and very delightful in the description of what he felt at the concert; the evening seemed to have been made up of exquisite moments. The moment of her stepping forward in the Octagon Room to speak to him, the moment of Mr. Elliot's appearing and tearing her away, and one or two subsequent moments, marked by returning hope or increasing despondency, were all dwelt on with energy.

' "To see you," he cried, "in the midst of those who could not be my well-wishers; to see your cousin close by you, conversing and smiling, and feel all the horrible eligibilities and proprieties of the match! To consider it as the certain wish of every being who could hope to influence you! Even if your own feelings were reluctant or indifferent, to consider what powerful support would be his! Was it not enough to make the fool of me which I appeared? How could I look on without agony? Was not the very sight of the friend who sat behind you; was not the recollection of what had been, the knowledge of her influence, the indelible, immovable impression of what persuasion had once done—was it not all against me?"

' "You should have distinguished," replied Anne, "You should not have suspected me now; the case so different, and my age so different . . ."

' "I was determined to see you again. My spirits rallied with the morning, and I felt that I had still a motive for remaining here . . . this would have been my last day in Bath."

'There was time for all this to pass, with such interruptions only as enhanced the charm of the communication, and Bath could hardly contain any other two beings at once so rationally and so rapturously happy as during that evening occupied the sofa of Mrs. Croft's drawing-room in Gay St.'

Jane Austen rejected this version of the reconciliation between Anne Elliot and Captain Wentworth. Was this because she felt it to be too close to real life? She may have decided that it betrayed the intimate feelings of one to whom she owed before everyone else her complete loyalty. And as an author, she may also have felt that it was not artistically suitable.

7. The Evidence—Emphasis on Emma

What felicity it is to hear a tune again
which has made one happy!—If I mistake
not that was danced at Weymouth.

JANE AUSTEN, *Persuasion*.

If we would continue Jane Austen's autobiography we shall not find it in *Persuasion*, after the cancelled chapter. That novel ends with the marriage of Anne Elliot and Frederick Wentworth and all goes smoothly. We have to look for something different—secrecy, tension, fitful happiness, anxiety, (and finally sorrow). John and Jane would realise after the bliss of their reconciliation at Bath that they cannot, for the present, announce their engagement or name the date of their wedding. John Wordsworth, although now commanding a great Indiaman, has still his fortune to make—he still cannot hope to be looked upon as a suitable husband for Jane. And so, very much against their own inclinations—they decide their re-engagement must be kept a secret.

As we have seen above in Chapter 6, this situation leads us to *Emma*—to Jane Fairfax and Frank Churchill. The whole story of Jane Fairfax's frustrations and difficult life—her poverty, the narrow limits of the Bates' home, her grandmother a clergy widow, and Miss Bates—are all a sort of caricature of what she, Jane Austen, may become. Then Jane Fairfax's fears and reluctance to become a governess are most deeply and personally felt. We have but to think of the circumstances of Jane Austen's life—the portionless daughter of

71

a poor clergyman, engaged to a poor sailor, to see the affinity between herself and Jane Fairfax.

There is an air of incomprehensible mystery about Jane Fairfax—she keeps in the shadows. Sometimes, for a fleeting moment we get a glimpse of the sun's rays full upon her and we feel we are about to pierce her secret, but it is, after all, only an oblique illumination and she passes from sight again, tantalising and intriguing. Jane Fairfax, and Jane Austen, endure what is almost unendurable for the sake of the man they love.

'You may well be amazed. But it is even so. There has been a solemn engagement between them ever since October, formed at Weymouth, and kept a secret from everybody. Not a creature knowing it but themselves—neither the Campbells, nor her family, nor his. It is so wonderful, that though perfectly convinced of the fact, it is yet almost incredible to myself. I can hardly believe it. I thought I knew him.'

Mrs. Weston had wished not to call on Jane Fairfax at all until Frank Churchill's uncle could be reconciled to the engagement's becoming known.

'. . . but Mr. Weston had thought differently; he was extremely anxious to shew his approbation to Miss Fairfax and her family, and did not conceive that any suspicion could be excited by it; or if it were, that it would be of any consequence; for "such things", he observed, "always got about." Emma smiled, and felt that Mr. Weston had very good reason for saying so. They had gone, in short—and very great had been the evident distress and confusion of the lady. She had hardly been able to speak a word, and every look and action had shown how deeply she was suffering from consciousness. Miss Fairfax's recent illness had offered a fair plea for Mrs. Weston to invite her to an airing; she had drawn back and declined at first, but on being pressed had yielded; and in the course of their drive, Mrs. Weston had, by gentle encouragement, overcome so much of her embarrassment, as to bring her to converse on the important subject. Apologies for her seemingly ungracious silence in their first reception, and the warmest expression of the gratitude she was always feeling towards herself and Mr. Weston, must necessarily open the cause; but these effusions were put by, they had talked a good deal of the present and of the future state of the engagement. Mrs. Weston was convinced that such conversation must be the greatest relief to her companion, pent up within her own mind as everything had so long been, and was very much pleased with all that she had said on the subject.

' "On the misery of what she had suffered, during the concealment of so many months," continued Mrs. Weston, "she was energetic. This was one of her expressions, 'I will not say, that since I entered into the engagement I have not had some happy moments; but I can honestly say, that I have never known the blessing of one tranquil hour:'—and the quivering lip, Emma, which uttered it, was an attestation that I felt at my heart."

' "Poor girl!" said Emma. "She thinks herself wrong, then, for having consented to a private engagement?"

' "Wrong!—No one, I believe, can blame her more than she is disposed to blame herself . . ."

' "Poor girl!" said Emma again. "She loves him then excessively, I suppose. It must have been from attachment only, that she could be led to form the engagement. Her affection must have overpowered her judgment."

' "Yes, I have no doubt of her being extremely attached to him . . ."

' ". . . You are very kind to bring me these interesting particulars. They show her to the greatest advantage. I am sure she is very good. I hope she will be very happy. It is fit that the fortune should be on his side, for I think the merit will be all on hers."

'Such a conclusion could not pass unanswered by Mrs. Weston. She thought well of Frank in almost every respect; and, what was more, she loved him very much, and her defence was, therefore, earnest. She talked with a good deal of reason, and at least equal affection . . .

'. . . Mrs. Weston's communications furnished Emma with more food for unpleasant reflection, by increasing her esteem and compassion, and her sense of past injustice towards Miss Fairfax . . . She must have been a perpetual enemy. They never could have been all three together, without her having stabbed Jane Fairfax's peace in a thousand instances; and on Box Hill, perhaps, it had been the agony of a mind that would bear no more.'

John Wordsworth returned to his Uncle's house at Windsor about mid-December, and it is most probable that they had become engaged before he left Jane Austen in Bath. Some of the feelings experienced by Jane Fairfax would have been felt by Jane during the coming months between December and May 1803, when John sailed on his second voyage as the Commander of *The Earl of Abergavenny*.

He writes to Dorothy from London, (Staple Inn) where he has returned by December 17th—he speaks of the childish ailments, and Mrs. Cookson has been fussing somewhat about them, and says: 'I do not believe they were ever in great danger.' He praises William's sonnet, on Bonaparte, but thinks he should not employ himself in that way.

Before he sailed that Spring, the Lowther debt had been paid to all the Wordsworth children. John wishes to invest his share and some of William's and Dorothy's in order to trade on a bigger scale than before. Before May 1803, he and Jane would try to meet again. In *Jane Austen, her life and Letters* by her great nephew and his son, William and Richard Austen-Leigh, we read: 'Our only evidence of Jane's having been absent from Bath in 1803 is that Sir Egerton Brydges,[1] in speaking of her, says: "The last time I think that I saw her was at Ramsgate in 1803".'

The *Life* also tells us that 'Francis Austen . . . on the Peace of Amiens, he, like many others, went on half-pay. His first employment when war broke out again, in 1803, was the raising from among the Kent fishermen of a corps of "sea fencibles", to protect the coast from invasion. His head-quarters were at Ramsgate, and it was quite likely that Jane would visit him there, especially if she could combine this visit with one to Godmersham.'

We must also take into account the probability of a visit by Jane Austen to her brother Henry and Eliza his wife, in London, at about this time. Ostensibly this visit was to negotiate the sale of her early novel *Susan* later *Northanger Abbey*[2]—and unwilling to appear under her own name— Henry's man of business, and a friend, Mr. Seymour, under-took the task for her. There would be good reason for Jane to need extra money for travelling, and other necessaries, in the early spring of 1803; she would wish to be near her future husband in the short time he had before sailing in May 1803.

He was obliged to be in London—he had a great deal of business on his hands—he gives typical examples of the kind of way his time is spent before a voyage in letters of the pre-vious year, to his sister Dorothy: 'I am obliged very often to be on board [at Gravesend] . . . when I am on board and clear of Gravesend, I shall write to you often. I am employed all day in shipping men, and with Tradesmen of every descrip-tion.'

A modern critic[3] has spoken of Jane Austen as a 'realist and a person who managed to live a very full life on very small means'. So we can be sure that the £10 she received in ex-change for her MS of *Susan* (*Northanger Abbey*), was stretched to the full. We can imagine her happiness, meeting John from her brother's house in London, when John would

75

be at Staple Inn[4] with Richard, or perhaps at his club. Later John would have been able to drive himself down to Ramsgate, a possible journey in the short time he had at his disposal, when Jane was there with Frank. Perhaps she was thinking of these meetings at the sailor brother's lodgings when she puts these words into Anne Elliot's mind at Lyme: 'There was so much attachment to Captain Wentworth in all this, and such a bewitching charm in a degree of hospitality so uncommon, so unlike the usual style of give and take invitations, and dinners of formality and display;' and again, later, she experiences more naval hospitality: 'they all went indoors . . . and found rooms so small as none but those who invite from the heart could think capable of accommodating so many;' and later Anne's (Jane's) enthusiasm for sailors is echoed in Louisa's rapturous words: 'of admiration and delight . . . their friendliness, their brotherliness, their openness, their uprightness; protesting that she was convinced of sailors having more worth and warmth than any other set of men in England; that they only knew how to live, and they only deserved to be respected and loved.'

When Jane writes of 'rooms so small as none but those who invite from the heart could think capable of accommodating so many' or 'a degree of hospitality so uncommon, so unlike the usual style of give and take invitations and dinners of formality and display,'—is she thinking of the contrast between her brothers Frank and Edward and their different ideas of hospitality, the one a country gentleman with an elegant seat at Godmersham Park, and the other a sailor living in cramped lodgings at Deal?

She writes, on a visit to Godmersham in October 1813: 'Here I am in Kent, with one brother [Edward] in the same county and another brother's wife [Mrs. Frank Austen], and see nothing of them—which seems unnatural—It will not last so for ever, I trust. I should like to have Mrs. Frank Austen and her children here for a week—but not a syllable of that nature is ever breathed.' She may too, have been thinking of the Wordsworths' first home at Dove Cottage, whose rooms were surely small enough to qualify, and where the invitations certainly came from the heart!

Jane clearly knew Ramsgate well. In *Mansfield Park*—in the description of Tom Bertram's mistake over the two Miss Sneyds, one being 'out', and the other still in the schoolroom, Tom says: 'I got into a dreadful scrape last year from want of them, [i.e. the close bonnet and demure air of the school-girl]. I went down to Ramsgate for a week with a friend last September, just after my return from the West Indies. My friend Sneyd—you have heard me speak of Sneyd, Edmund; his father and mother and sisters were there, all new to me. When we reached Albion Place, they were out; we went after them and found them on the pier.'

Ramsgate is also mentioned in *Pride and Prejudice* at the end of Chapter 35, in Darcy's letter to Elizabeth Bennet, where he exposes Wickham's true character—telling her, among his other sins, of Wickham's attempted elopement with Darcy's young sister, aged fifteen, Georgiana, then residing at Ramsgate with a governess.

Ramsgate, then, may have been a scene of John and Jane's first rambles to the sea together after their re-engagement. John would most likely drive himself there from Gravesend, or London, in his own gig. They probably made one or two excursions into the surrounding countryside, perhaps to Minster, with its beautiful ancient Norman Church, in the short spells of free time he would have before sailing. The fishing village, grown into a little port in the mid-eighteenth century, was a convenient refuge for ships sailing through the Downs on their way down the Channel, so that there may have been a further meeting between them, if *The Earl of Abergavenny* anchored in the Downs, and John came ashore.

Captain Wordsworth sailed in May 1803, and returned to England in August 1804. Did Jane Austen go down to Portsmouth, when the Indiaman anchored there, before leaving? She is said to have surprised Admiral Foote that she 'had the power of drawing the Portsmouth scene so well.'[5] In *Mansfield Park* the vividness of the description of the Sunday walk on the ramparts is incomparably lovely:

'Mrs. Price took her weekly walk on the ramparts every fine Sunday throughout the year, always going after morning service and staying till dinner-time. It was her public place; there she met her acquaintance, heard a little news, talked over the badness of the Portsmouth servants, and wound up her spirits for the six days ensuing.

'Thither they now went; Mr. Crawford most happy to consider the Miss Prices as his peculiar charge; the day was uncommonly lovely. It was really March; but it was April in its mild air, brisk soft wind, and bright sun, but occasionally clouded for a minute; and every thing looked so beautiful under the influence of such a sky, the effects of the shadows pursuing each other, on the ships at Spithead and the island beyond, with the ever-varying hues of the sea now at high-water, dancing in its glee and dashing against the ramparts with so fine a sound, produced altogether such a combination of charms for Fanny, as made her gradually careless of the circumstances under which she felt them.'

'The island beyond'—the Isle of Wight was beloved by both Jane Austen and John Wordsworth. In *Mansfield Park* Fanny is spoken of by her cousins, Maria and Julia: 'She thinks of nothing but the Isle of Wight, and calls it The Island, as if there were no other island in the world;' and the island crops up several times in Jane's letters, and always with the same appreciation.

John Wordsworth must often have visited the Isle of Wight while waiting to sail at Portsmouth. As he was a North-countryman, he would not call it 'The Island'—as a Hampshire native would do. In a letter to Dorothy from Portsmouth, April 2nd, 1801, he says: 'I have been on shore this afternoon to stretch my legs upon the Isle of Wight, the primroses are beautiful and the daisies after sunset are like little white stars upon the dark green fields . . .'

In the spring of 1803 it is possible that John and Jane Austen were able to meet on the Island. There is a pastoral romantic beauty about the Isle of Wight, still to be found in some parts to-day. Jane's friends the Biggs, were connected by marriage with the Blachfords (of Osborne), and she also had family ties with the island through her mother's family, the Leighs, and possibly John had naval friends there too. In his log book he writes, May 17th: 'Weighed and run into the clear birts and anchored near Bembridge.' 'May 19th—weighed and run out.'

The call at Bembridge (Brading) Harbour was for the purpose of taking on a supply of fresh water for the voyage. John would be able to stretch his legs, and visit Jane while this was being done. The Hills owned the Manor of Shanklin and Bonchurch. At the latter place they had, in the eighteenth century, converted a farm house into a charming 'gentleman's residence'—a secluded holiday 'cottage' with a thatched roof.

A local historian, Pennant, says of it: 'St. Boniface Cottage is an elegant little building under the precipitous rocks. We were introduced into it, and met with a most polite reception from Mrs. Hill, the lady of Colonel Hill, the owner, who made this most sequestered spot her frequent and long abode.'

And a Mr. Wyndham also said of it: '. . . a comfortable house, and lies at the foot of a steep mountainous down, on a little level plain and looks towards some long regular slopes of rock, naturally covered with coppices, and between which a few partial views of the sea open to the house.' The writer of a guide to the Isle of Wight, Hassell, says, in 1790: 'It is so retired that it might almost be styled a hermitage; and at the same time it boasts of all that Nature can bestow.'

The Hills of Bonchurch and Shanklin were related to Southey's mother's family; (Southey's uncle, Dr. Hill later married Catherine Bigg, the Austens' friend) the Shanklin Hills were also distant kinsman of the Leighs, Jane's mother's family. So that it is possible that Jane, perhaps with Cassandra, would have been staying at St. Boniface House during the spring of 1803, when John was making his final preparations at Portsmouth, and calling at Bembridge on his way to sea. We know that Jane Awdry, Catherine's elder sister, and her husband, Sir John Awdry, took the house during 1810–1811, and so it is possible they rented it at an earlier date, or other members of that family, or connections of the Austens—for Jane to stay with there.

We know that she loved the house, for in a letter—written years after—she refers to it as: 'That sweet St. Boniface House' as though she had nostalgic memories of her own visit to it. And John—riding at dusk from Bembridge to Bonchurch to be with her, would see the daisies in the dark green fields 'like little white stars'—these, the larger, marguerite kind, do not close their petals at night, and so would show up as he rode past the fields to St. Boniface House, in the dusk of that May evening. Arriving at 'that sweet St. Boniface House' he dismounts and leaving his horse to graze, he tethers it to the old ring in the garden wall, and Jane, on the watch from the upper windows of the house, runs eagerly down to greet him for their time is short. Their host and hostess, knowing their secret—leave them, as much as possible, to themselves that one evening.

In the morning they may have taken the footpath from Ventnor, over St. Boniface Down, towards Appuldurcombe House, the beautiful Palladian home of the Worsleys.[6] It would be misty still, on a May morning, and the view seawards not at all clear. But they walked on, absorbed in the present happiness of being alone together. There is a passage in Jane Austen's last novel, the fragmentary *Sanditon* which, to readers who know the walk Jane and John *may* have taken from St. Boniface House to Appuldurcombe House, must clearly have been in the author's mind as she wrote.

'The road to Sanditon House was a broad, handsome planted approach, between fields, and conducting at the end of a quarter of a mile through second gates into the grounds, which though not extensive had all the beauty and respectability which an abundance of very fine timber could give. These entrance gates were so much in a corner of the grounds or Paddock so near one of its boundaries, that an outside fence was at first almost pressing on the road—till an angle here, and a curve there threw them to a better distance. The fence was a proper park paling in excellent condition; with clusters of fine elms, or rows of old thorns following its line almost everywhere. Almost must be stipulated—for there were vacant spaces—and through one of these, Charlotte as soon as they entered the enclosure, caught a glimpse over the pales of something white and womanish in the field on the other side; —it was something which immediately brought Miss B. into her head—and stepping to the pales, she saw indeed—and very decidedly, in spite of the mist; Miss B. seated, not far before her, at the foot of the bank which sloped down from the outside of the paling—and which a narrow path seemed to skirt along;—Miss Brereton seated, apparently very composedly—and Sir E. D. by her side. They were sitting so near each other and appeared so closely engaged in gentle conversation, that Charlotte instantly felt she had nothing to do but step back again, and say not a word. Privacy was certainly their object . . . Among other points of moralising reflection which the sight of this tête à tête produced, Charlotte could not but think of the extreme difficulty which secret lovers must have in a proper spot for their stolen interviews. Here perhaps they had thought themselves so perfectly secure from observation!—the whole field open before them—a steep bank and pales never crossed by foot of man at their back— a great thickness of air in aid. Yet here, she had seen them. They were really ill-used . . .'

So they talked—of John's coming voyage, of their plans for their future life together, of the time, not long they hoped and prayed, when John could retire from the sea and live in modest comfort with Jane, and once again take up the quiet pursuits of a country life which they both so much enjoyed. John would speak of William's advice as to books, in answer to John's enquiry as to what he should take for a voyage of sixteen months in addition to his volume of Shakespeare. John had sent up to Grasmere his set of Anderson's poets, which William had asked to borrow; since John only wished for Spenser William advised him to buy a separate copy containing Spenser's 'State of Ireland' in addition to the poems, if it can be obtained. He also recommends Milton's Sonnets; John speaks of enjoying his reading of Shakespeare, especially *Othello*, though the ending is very different from the productions he has seen of it. He speaks of having, 'been several times to the play since I came to London—the houses are so large that you can hear nothing and I think we shall never see another play well acted upon the London stage—the favourite Pizarro is beautiful in the scenery, but the noise, rant and ham acting—(excessively)—is disgusting—Shakespeare's plays are not liked by the town—the reason I conceive to be that many of the beautiful passages are not heard and understood—the house being so large and I think too a great deal must be lost in the acting.'

As they walked, they spoke of modern poetry, of Coleridge, and of the latest volume of William's poems,[7] and Jane pleases John with her appreciation of the same poems as he loves—

they both feel William 'has the true soul of poetry'. Their families come into their conversation, Jane speaking of the children of her brothers, the Godmersham family, and then the sailor brothers' children. John describes the children at Forncett, and how fond he is of them and believes he became a great favourite with them; 'George, the youngest boy, when I was walking with him in the garden the morning before I came away, got a rope and with the assistance of his little sister, would tie me to a tree and said I should not go away so soon!'

So the precious few hours glide away and all too soon John leaves on his return ride—where he is rowed out to the waiting Indiaman 'anchored near Bembridge'.

Jane, left behind, walked back to St. Boniface House. Early next morning, accompanied by Cassandra, she climbed St. Boniface Down, and there seating herself on a grassy bank, with an old thorn bush as a shelter from the breezes blowing in from the sea, she watched the China Fleet and its convoying man of war sail away out of sight. The great Indiaman *The Earl of Abergavenny* she would easily distinguish among them—and picture her beloved Commander on board—'looking perhaps towards the very point of where she then was'.[8]

We can get an idea of Jane's vigil and of her appearance, if we examine the coloured drawing signed and dated by Cassandra Austen, and described years later by Anna Lefroy as 'a sketch which Aunt Cassandra made of her in one of their expeditions—sitting down out of doors on a hot day, with her bonnet strings untied'. She gazed out to sea until 'the very truck of the last topmast stole away'—her 'lip quivered as she murmured, without removing her wet eyes from the vacant and solemn horizon, "They that go down to the sea in ships, that do business in great waters—these see the works of the Lord, and His wonders in the deep".'[8]

From May 1803 until his return in August 1804, Jane

would be following in imagination all John's movements, as far as she could glean them from his letters sent back to her from the various ports of call and from the newspapers. We must feel the last lines of *Persuasion* describe her completely at this time:

'Anne was tenderness itself, and she had the full worth of it in Captain Wentworth's affection. His profession was all that could ever make her friends wish that tenderness less; she gloried in being a sailor's [future] wife, but she must pay the tax of quick alarms for belonging to that profession.'

'Quick alarms' Jane would certainly have known[9]—if the news of the encounter with Admiral Linois' Squadron reached her earlier that summer. She might have feared for John's safety in the engagement with the French—the 'touch with the Great Nation'. But the full details of this affair, surely one of the most astonishing in the whole of the war, of the defeat, the rout, of a French Squadron, under its Admiral by a British Merchant fleet which was by comparison lightly armed, would not be known until the detailed report was sent in by the senior Commander, Captain Nathaniel Dance of the East India Company's ship, *Earl Camden*. His letter was written on board, and dated August 8th, 1804 as the fleet arrived safely in the Channel.[10]

There is a letter from John Wordsworth also written on August 8th to his cousin, Captain John Wordsworth, the former commander of the *Abergavenny*, and now living at Brougham Hall, near Penrith, Westmorland. John speaks of the voyage just completed and of the safe arrival, under convoy of H.M. ship *The Plantagenet*, of the whole of the China Fleet, with not a ship lost and very little damage; he speaks of Admiral Linois' attack, saying the *Abergavenny* is unhurt.

It is a typically modest letter, making little of the stirring event. He does not mention the commendation of his senior Commander, Captain Dance, who wrote:

'In justice to my fellow commanders, I must state, that every ship was cleared and prepared for action; and as I had communication with almost all of them during the two days we were in presence of the enemy, I found them unanimous in the determined resolution to defend the valuable property entrusted to their charge to the last extremity, with a full conviction of the successful event of their exertions; and this spirit was fully seconded by the gallant officers and ships' companies.'

The next letter to his cousin Captain Wordsworth is dated August 15th; this time it contains news of the efforts he has been making to secure a good voyage for his next venture, the Bengal and China he hopes to get, which is considered the first of the service. Between these two letters a week has elapsed, and it is safe to imagine that John spent some part of that time in being re-united with Jane. Their meeting took place, perhaps somewhere on the coast, where with her brother Henry and his wife Eliza, and Cassandra, for some of the time she has been enjoying summer rambles. In a letter dated 8th April, 1805, to Cassandra, Jane says: 'Henry talks of the rambles we took together (on the sea-coast) last summer with pleasing affection . . .'

In *Persuasion* Captain Harville tells Anne Elliot: 'if I could make you comprehend what a man suffers when he takes a last look at his wife and children, and watches the boat that he has sent them off in, as long as it is in sight, and then turns away and says, "God knows whether we ever meet again!" And then, if I could convey to you the glow of his soul when he does see them again; when, coming back after a twelvemonth's absence perhaps, and obliged to put into another port, he calculates how soon it be possible to get them there, pretending to deceive himself, saying, "They cannot be here till such a day," but all the while hoping for them twelve hours sooner, and seeing them arrive at last, as if Heaven had

given them wings, by many hours sooner still! If I could explain to you all this, and all that a man can bear and do, and
glories to do for the sake of these treasures of his existence!
I speak you know, only of such men as have hearts! pressing
his own with emotion.'

John Wordsworth too would have felt that same 'glow of
his soul' when he saw Jane after his long, eventful absence of
almost sixteen months. We cannot know for certain where
that meeting was—perhaps at the Island again—but wherever
it was, it seems certain it must have been before the China
Fleet finally docked round at Gravesend; perhaps it is safest
to think they met somewhere on the Channel coast. That Jane
often, during her rambles with her family that summer of
1804 'on the sea-coast' sat looking out to sea, searching the
horizon for the returning fleet, exactly as she did the spring
before, when the ships left, we need be in no doubt. And
Cassandra's coloured sketch of her, 'sitting down out of doors
on a hot day, with her bonnet strings untied' is dated 1804,
but can be thought of as an adequate representation of Jane
in either year.

There would almost certainly have been receptions[11] got up
in honour of the return of the China Fleet, and some of these
John Wordsworth would feel bound to attend. No doubt some
of these were held at Weymouth. There are several references
to Weymouth in *Emma*, and for these tantalisingly brief
moments we are onlookers—at a distance, seeing, imperfectly,
the gay and lively society at this fashionably old-fashioned
Royal resort, favourite of George III, his Queen and family.

In *Emma*, when Frank Churchill eventually comes to stay
with his father and his step-mother at Highbury (and it was
not till Jane Fairfax herself was also there), one of his first
visits is to the Bates's, where Jane Fairfax is living with her
Grandmother and Aunt. He asks for directions to the house:
' "To be sure we do," cried his father: "Miss Bates—we

passed her house—I saw Miss Bates at the window. True, true, you are acquainted with Miss Fairfax; I remember you knew her at Weymouth, and a fine girl she is. Call upon her, by all means."

' "There is no necessity for my calling this morning," said the young man; "another day would do as well; but there was that degree of acquaintance at Weymouth which———" '

Later, Emma, to Frank Churchill: ' "I merely asked whether you had known much of Miss Fairfax and her party at Weymouth."

' "And now that I understand your question, I must pronounce it to be a very unfair one. It is always the lady's right to decide on the degree of acquaintance. Miss Fairfax must already have given her account. I shall not commit myself by claiming more than she may choose to allow."

' "Upon my word! You answer as discreetly as she could do herself. But her account of everything leaves so much to be guessed, she is so very reserved, so very unwilling to give the least information about anybody, that I really think you may say what you like of your acquaintance with her."

' "May I indeed? Then I will speak the truth, and nothing suits me so well. I met her frequently at Weymouth. I had known the Campbells a little in town; and at Weymouth we were very much in the same set. Colonel Campbell is a very agreeable man, and Mrs. Campbell a friendly, warm-hearted woman. I like them all." '

Later, in Chapter 25, Emma again has a conversation with Frank Churchill about Jane Fairfax:

' "And then he [Mr. Dixon] saved her life. Did you ever hear of that? A water party; and by some accident she was falling overboard. He caught her." "He did. I was there—one of the party." '

By a most fortunate coincidence, there is an account of just such a water-party which took place at Weymouth in 1804,

written in her diary by a contemporary of Jane Austen's—
Miss Elizabeth Ham.[12]

She says: 'Of all visiting, these parties on ship-board were
then the most delightful. The little anxiety about the weather
enhanced the pleasure of a fine day, then the excitement of
getting on board. There was something particularly exhilara-
ting in the long, well-timed sweep of the eighteen-oared barge
over the dancing waters, then the petits soins of the blue-
coated beaux, wrapping boat-cloaks and bunting round the
ladies' feet. Then being safely tucked in the commodious chair
to be hoisted on board, when timid young ladies used to affect
still more timidity than naturally belonged to them . . .

'The weather was propitious, the barge waiting for us. The
deck of the ship converted into a Saloon for dancing by means
of tarpaulin lined with flags. By striking away the stanchions
between decks a good spring was given to the floor, considered
a great advantage in the spirited jumping days of Country
Dances. The cool sea-breezes made these temporary Ball-rooms
quite delightful and refreshing, very different from the pent-in
atmosphere of a closed room on shore.'

There are other references to Weymouth in *Emma*. Jane
Fairfax is playing the Coles's new piano at their party at
Highbury—and Emma listens; 'Frank Churchill sang again.
They had sung together once or twice, it appeared, at Wey-
mouth . . .'

And again, when Jane Fairfax's new pianoforte—and its
mysterious donor, are under discussion:

' "Whoever Colonel Campbell might employ," said Frank
Churchill, "the person has not chosen ill. I heard a good deal
of Colonel Campbell's taste at Weymouth; and the softness
of the upper notes I am sure is exactly what he and all that
party would particularly prize . . ." He went to the pianoforte, and begged Miss Fairfax, who was still sitting at it, to
play something more.

' "If you are very kind", said he, "it will be one of the waltzes we danced last night; let me live them over again . . ."

'She played—[and he said] "What felicity it is to hear a tune again which has made one happy! If I mistake not that was danced at Weymouth."

'She looked up at him for a moment, coloured deeply, and played something else.'

We must feel that these Weymouth scenes in *Emma* are deeply felt, have a personal ring about them. But they remain mysterious. If Jane and John *did* meet on these social occasions at Weymouth—and perhaps they might have done at Belfield House—they too may have had to seem to be only acquaintances.

There is only one letter of Jane Austen's of 1804, and it does not add much to our knowledge of her movements. It is dated Friday, September 14th, and it is from Lyme. By this date John Wordsworth is back in London. Jane's letter, to Cassandra, is not a happy one. She is in lodgings with her parents and sounds lonely, with no particular companions. Cassandra, who has just left them, has been to Weymouth, and is now on her way to the Lloyds at Hurstbourne, where Martha is nursing the ailing Mrs. Lloyd.

It seems likely that Jane and Cassandra have exchanged places—Jane has been rambling with the Henry Austens along the sea-coast, and probably also visiting Weymouth for a short time, as we have seen above, (although Cassandra may not have known of this). Cassandra meanwhile has been with her parents at Lyme. Jane's references to Weymouth in her letter are not, of course, to be taken seriously, and she makes a little fun of Cassandra's general disapproval of the town.

'Weymouth is altogether a shocking place, I perceive, without recommendation of any kind, and worthy only of being frequented by the inhabitants of Gloucester . . .'—that is, only of being worthy to receive the annual visits of the inhabitants of Gloucester Lodge [The King and Queen, and Royal Family]. The letter goes on 'I am really very glad we did not go there, and that Henry and Eliza saw nothing in it to make them feel differently.' Jane is very glad that her parents decided against Weymouth as a place for a family holiday— and her remark about Henry and Eliza shows that they too would feel it was too lively, and expensive, for this purpose. The Austens would prefer the less fashionable and more peaceful atmosphere of Lyme.

John Wordsworth, meanwhile, is in London and by mid-September has obtained the promise of the voyage he so much wished for. He writes to his sister Dorothy to tell her of the success of his efforts: his letter is dated September 12th, 1804. He tells Dorothy he has a Bombay and China nomination for his next voyage, which has been handed to Mr. Dent for him, by Sir Francis Baring, the East India Company Chairman. John tells of his great anxiety while all the negotiations have been afoot to get it for him, and goes on: 'I have been ill and well, well and ill, according as my hopes have been rais'd or depress'd.' William Wilberforce has been a good friend to him in all this, and is 'a friend and fellow-labourer in the same vineyard with Mr. Grant', (a chairman of the East India Company's Directors. He and Wilberforce both wished to secure the free entry of Christian Missionaries to India).[13]

John concludes by saying he is sorry not to be able to come north to see them before he sails, but he is too busy preparing for the voyage, and cannot leave London. There is another letter of September 15th to his cousin, Captain John senior, giving him the good news of having obtained the Bengal and China voyage; he writes to him again on October 12th, giving him details of the work he is doing in preparation for the great voyage. John tells his cousin that he is sending up some pipes of wine, tea and a 'handsome China set for Mrs. Wordsworth'.

There are no further letters from John until January 23rd, 1805—when he writes again to his cousin—from on board *The Earl of Abergavenny*, now arrived at Portsmouth.

Between October and January we must imagine that he was rarely able to have any very long spells of leisure, for visits to friends, and in his last letter to William, dated January 24th, he speaks of only having been three miles out of London since his return. But there would certainly have been opportunities for John and Jane to meet again, most likely in London itself. Jane would be able to stay in London, with Henry and Eliza. The possibility of a farewell meeting on the coast would have to be ruled out at that time of year, and the sudden illness and death of Mr. Austen towards the end of January 1805, makes Jane's presence at home in Bath a certainty.

Of their lives together, there is not much more to be told. In the autumn and winter of 1804–5, and up to the time of the sailing of the *Abergavenny* in January 1805, John Wordsworth was caught up in the bustle of preparation, and, no doubt, reluctantly, into a certain amount of social life in London which his promotion to the 'best voyage in the service' would inevitably lead him. There can have been little time for peaceful country walks and talks, with Jane on literary subjects, especially poetry, and also exchange of news of their two families. When William, in his elegiac poem on his brother 'To the Daisy', says:

> 'That he, who had been cast
> Upon a way of life unmeet
> for such a gentle soul and sweet . . .'

he means this stifling of all John's real interests—his love of nature, of all quiet things, and instead, having to throw himself into a life which was hectic, competitive and something of a social whirl, among the rich merchant 'princes' of the

East India Company and their contacts in the east. In this context it is interesting to note that John was a member of Brook's Club at this time—and in the account for goods supplied to him, silk stockings are a necessary item. As well, it was also unmeet for such a gentle soul, such as we know John to have been, to have to discipline his sailors, using the rough justice of the day. An example can be found in his log book:

'March 28th, 1801–2. Punished John Martin[14] with 2 dozen lashes for insolence, drunkenness and striking the 4th Officer.'

So perhaps we can guess at the yearning of John, of them both, as they bid each other farewell, in those weeks at the end of the year (1804) looking beyond this present hectic time, towards the peace and delight of a safe anchorage, a home of their own together. Dorothy's description of her 'little parsonage' with William, written years before, in 1793, to her friend Jane Marshall, may contain something of John and Jane's vision of home: 'I have laid the particular scheme of happiness for each season. When I think of winter I hasten to furnish our little parlour, I close the shutters, set out the tea-table, brighten the fire. When our refreshment is ended I produce our work, and William brings his books to our table and contributes at once to our instruction and amusement, and at intervals we lay aside the book and each hazard our observations upon what has been read without fear of ridicule or censure. We talk over past days, we do not sigh for any pleasures beyond our humble habitation "The central point of all our joys".'

When John speaks of travelling only three miles out of London since his return in August 1804, he may not have counted (perhaps because of the need to keep their engagement a secret) his rides down to Bookham, in Surrey, to see Jane. Mrs. Cooke, Mrs. George Austen's first cousin, was married to the Rector of Great Bookham; there were three children, now adult, Theophilus, George and Mary, and Jane

Austen was a great favourite with them all. At this time she may have accepted one of the many pressing invitations to visit Bookham Rectory.

Great Bookham is a pleasant village, with its church dating back in part to the 11th century, and with a number of interesting old cottages in the High Street. The Rectory, a Georgian house would have seemed a peaceful haven to both John Wordsworth and Jane Austen in their brief visits as guests of the Cookes. It was, and still is, an interesting neighbourhood both for the natural beauties of the landscape, and for its houses of different periods, with their parks and grounds. The road past Bookham Church leads to the richly wooded Bookham Common, and on to Slyfield House, a fine Jacobean mansion; then there are the beauties of Boxhill close at hand, the charm of the Mole valley to be explored, and Mickleham, where, at nearby Juniper Hall, a party of French emigrés took refuge— among them, Fanny Burney's future husband, General D'arblay. Perhaps it is not unlikely that Henry and Eliza Austen, who would have travelled with Jane to Bookham Rectory from London, would go on to visit friends at Juniper Hall.

So perhaps it is in this neighbourhood that we may get some of the exquisite pastoral 'feel' of the outdoor scenes in *Emma*. Scenes where country sights and sounds fill the hearts of the onlookers with peace. These passages from the Donwell Abbey excursion are typical: 'They . . . followed one another to the delicious shade of a broad short avenue of limes, which stretching beyond the garden at an equal distance from the river, seemed the finish of the pleasure grounds . . . it was in itself a charming walk, and the view which closed it extremely pretty. The considerable slope, at nearly the foot of which the Abbey stood, gradually acquired a steeper form beyond its grounds; and at half a mile distance was a bank of considerable abruptness and grandeur, well clothed with wood;—and at

93

the bottom of this bank, favourably placed and sheltered, rose the Abbey Mill Farm, with meadows in front, and the river making a close and handsome curve around it.

'It was a sweet view—sweet to the eye and the mind. English verdure, English culture, English comfort, seen under a sun bright, without being oppressive . . . with all its appendages of prosperity and beauty, its rich pastures, spreading flocks, orchard in bloom, and light column of smoke ascending.'

It is not difficult to picture the lovers walking in tranquil surroundings such as these, and, through the depth of their love for one another, they were able to surmount the difficulties of the present, and the harsh necessity of their parting, and attain an inner peace which no storms hereafter could ever do away. But before reaching this stage in their love, they were to meet difficulties, to stumble—and the Boxhill episode in *Emma* seems to hint at something of the kind. The atmosphere of pastoral serenity evaporates completely at the end of the Donwell strawberry picnic. This love of 'English verdure' is missing in Frank Churchill's petulant speech to Emma, coming late from his aunt at Richmond—to join them all at Donwell. He finds Emma and Mr. Woodhouse indoors 'looking over views in Switzerland'.

' "As soon as my aunt gets well, I shall go abroad," said he. "I shall never be easy till I have seen some of these places. You will have my sketches, some time or other, to look at—or my tour to read—or my poem. I shall do something to expose myself."

' "Your uncle and aunt will never allow you to leave England."

' "They may be induced to go too. A warm climate may be prescribed for her. I have more than half an expectation of our all going abroad. I assure you I have. I feel a strong persuasion, this morning, that I shall soon be abroad. I ought to travel. I am tired of doing nothing. I want change. I am serious, Miss Woodhouse, whatever your penetrating eye may fancy—I am sick of England—and would leave it to-morrow, if I could." '

The same party arrange to go to Boxhill on the next day. But there is a tension in the air which cannot be overcome, in spite of everything being favourable to happiness.

'They had a very fine day for Boxhill; and all other outward circumstances of arrangement, accommodation, and punctuality, were in favour of a pleasant party . . . Nothing was wanting but to be happy when they got there. Seven miles were travelled in expectation of enjoyment, and everybody had a burst of admiration on first arriving; but in the general amount of the day there was a deficiency. There was a langour, a want of spirits, a want of union, which could not be got over . . .' When they all sat down it was better; to her [Emma's] taste a great deal better, for Frank Churchill grew talkative and gay . . . and Emma, glad to be enlivened, not sorry to be flattered, was gay and easy too, and gave him all the friendly encouragement to be gallant, which she had ever given in the first and most animating period of their acquaintance; but which now, in her own estimation, meant nothing, though in the judgment of most people looking on it must have had such an appearance as no English word but flirtation could very well describe.'

The cloud over the scene on Boxhill does not lift; it deepens, and ends in Mr. Knightley's reproof, and Emma's tears. That this scene on Boxhill is autobiographical cannot be claimed. But that there are in it aspects of a similar situation having taken place seems likely. The whole atmosphere has a personal ring. It can be explained by Jane's misery at John's impending departure, and his gloomy reserve because he is overfatigued with his recent exacting work for his voyage, and then the long ride down to Bookham.

As it was unlikely they were known to be engaged (except

to Henry, and Mrs. Cooke) it is probable that Theophilus
Cooke, the elder of the two boy cousins—would keep up his
usual gay, bantering chatter with Jane; she says, in after
years, of him : 'he came back in time to show his usual ,noth-
ing meaning, harmless, heartless, civility . . .' If he showed it
to Jane at this time, when John's nerves were stretched and
tense, it would have been a strong contribution to a return
of jealousy in him, and seems a likely explanation of the
gloom and langour of the scene as a whole.

It is also true to say—as Miss Brophy has observed in her
introductory essay to *Pride and Prejudice* (Pan paperback
edition, 1967), that the qualities of Jane Austen's men and
women are sometimes interchangeable : 'Certainly Jane
Austen did not consider Elizabeth's high fantasy and spirits
specifically feminine, since they turn up reincarnated in Henry
Tilney before changing sex back into Emma. So that when
Jane Fairfax tormented and sad at witnessing what seems to
be a flirtation between Frank and Emma at Boxhill, can bear
it no longer, and turns to her aunt, and says : 'Now, Ma'am
shall we join Mrs. Elton?' she *is* John Wordsworth, having
his feeling and reactions strained in a similar way, when Jane
Austen speaks to either Theophilus or George Cooke, with
the light-hearted gaiety which masks the misery and
poignancy of her own feelings, as Frank does in this scene on
Boxhill.

There is in existence to-day an oil painting[15] on panel the
subject of which reminds one of the mysterious pastoral
quality of *Emma*, and its pair of secret, star-cross'd lovers.
The picture was probably painted by a Flemish artist resident
in England during the Commonwealth. It is of 'an alfresco
meal, served in the shade of a fine house, prepared for several
guests'. The subject of the painting can be taken as a straight-
forward scene of a pleasant social occasion of a party of friends
eating and drinking out of doors on a summer's day. But there

is a hidden meaning—and the picture is of importance because of it. The reason for speaking of it here is to focus attention on the background of the picture:

'In the distance . . . an affectionate couple enter a delightful garden, like the fringe of the garden of the Hesperides. They both seem remote, and have nothing to do with the diners . . . Are the figures about to enter the garden, through the gateway with its cherubim keystone, to symbolise the hoped for freedom, perhaps not on earth, for the couple?'

8. The Evidence from Other Sources

She would dwell on such dead themes,
not as one who remembers,
But rather as one who sees . . .

THOMAS HARDY, One We Knew.

John writes of very bad weather in his letter to his cousin, Captain Wordsworth,[1] written when he arrives at Portsmouth on January 23rd, 1805. *The Warren Hastings* has been in collision with *The Abergavenny* in the Downs, on their way; the accident was caused by a gale through poor visibility, and snow and sleet from Gravesend to Portsmouth. He speaks of feeling unwell—but says *The Abergavenny* has suffered little damage. He writes again on the 28th to the same; their convoy is to be the frigate *Weymouth*—of 44 guns. He cannot sail yet as the gale is still blowing. The carpenters are busy with the repairs—and the rat-catcher is on board. Again on January 31st, he writes to his cousin, then staying at Mascall's Hotel, Adelphi, London, telling him of a fair wind; they are to proceed to sea to-morrow.

'The Commodore intends to go through the Needles, a passage I do not like much but hope will be attended with no accident . . . I am very much pleased with all my passengers. Captain Hippisley whom you perhaps remember at Bath, at least he knews you, Commands the troops, he seems to be a very moderate and sensible man and I like him much. Mr. Evans and his family are moderate in their wishes and expectations, and seemed to be pleased with me and the ship.

Mr. Routhedge is as good and quiet a man as ever booked a passage in an Indiaman.

'Indeed I think we shall do as far beyond my highest expectations, I mean when we get clear of the land and a little settled, if we do not, I fear it will be my fault.

'I am little used to company and shall feel myself not at home at the first but I trust that will soon wear off. Give my kindest remembrances to Mrs. Wordsworth,

I am, dear Cousin,

Yours very affectionately,

J. W.'

John writes a last letter to his brother:

Ship *Abergavenny* at
Portsmouth.
January 24th, 1805.

'My dear William,

'I ought to have written to you long ago, but I have a most utter dislike to writing if I can avoid it, and I can assure you, tho' no man of business myself, I have had quite enough to engage the attention of a man more fitted for it than myself ... I have got my investment upon the best of terms, having paid ready money for it, which I was enabled to do by one gentleman lending me £5,000. It amounts to about £20,000, in goods and money. The passengers are all down, and we are anxiously expecting to sail. We shall muster at my table 36 or 38 persons. This must alone have given me a great deal of trouble to provide provisions, etc. for them. I was obliged to apply to the Court of Directors to have some of the passengers turned out of the ship, which was granted. I thought at one time I should have had 45 persons at my table.

'In ship's company we have 200, and soldiers and passengers 200 more, amounting altogether to 400, so that I shall have sufficient employment on my hands to keep all these people in order.

'I should have liked very much to have seen the poetry you have written (which I have not seen). In the *Lyrical Ballads* my favourites are 'The Mad Mother', part of 'The Indian Woman', and 'Joanna'; I like 'Michael' and all the poems on the naming of places, but 'Joanna' best, and I also like 'The Brothers'—(a seal tear here). The poem on The Wye is a poem that I admire, but after reading it I do not like to turn to it again. Among those unpublished that I have seen my favourite is 'The Leech Gatherer', 'The Sparrow's Nest', 'The Butterfly' and 'The Cuckow'. There is a harshness in many of the rest which I do not like. I think the *Lyrical Ballads* taken all together far superior to the last poems.

'Remember me most affectionately to Mary and Dorothy. Give my little namesake and his sister a kiss from me, and believe me to be,

Your affectionate brother,
John Wordsworth.

'Address: Wm. Wordsworth, Esq., Ambleside, Westmorland.

So John left England and all those dear to him in high hopes of a successful voyage. On February 5th he was dead.

The report of the loss of *The Earl of Abergavenny* in the *Gentleman's Magazine* for 1805 and other newspapers of that date give a false impression of the details of the tragedy. These reports imply that the guns were not fired soon enough to summon help, and that the Captain of the vessel made no effort to save himself. This heaped distress on his family and friends, and Charles Lamb worked indefatigably to remove all doubts from their minds as to the true details of those last hours of John's life, and to post them up to William, Mary and Dorothy, as soon as he could. From his work as a clerk in the India House, he was able to do this, but he also got information direct from passengers and crew who had been saved. Jane Austen may not have had an opportunity of reading these accurate reports of the East India Company's findings after the official enquiry. Yet it is likely that William would have written direct to her. (Details of the evidence of T. Gilpin have been given in an earlier chapter.)

It is interesting here to quote from the letter of a Mrs. King-Warry, sent to Miss Catherine Maclean in 1932, when she was writing her book on Dorothy Wordsworth.[1] Mrs. King-Warry is herself an old lady at the time of her letter:

'. . . looking back to my childhood, and listening to the story from my grandmother of the finding of John Wordsworth's body, and the burials in Wyke churchyard. This wreck on the dreaded Shambles—touched the Islanders [Portland] even more than other losses—I was never tired of hearing these tales—on stormy nights mostly, with the long drawn swish of "Dylan's death groan" echoing amongst the rocks and was taught to utter childish petitions for the "poor souls at sea" . . . I thought you might like to hear a reference to the loss of *The Earl of Abergavenny* first hand.'

These were told by her grandmother—born in 1782—and coming herself from a long line of sea captains, the Pearces, she was naturally sympathetic to disasters at sea. 'It was Captain Wordsworth's good seamanship which got her off the Shambles . . . A nephew of my Grandmother—Captain Richard Pearce—discussing John Wordsworth's seamanship with her—said he rated it very highly . . .'

'I shall never forget the general impression of the story on my childish mind—more from the awed, hushed tone of my Grandmother's voice than the actual tragedy which I was too young to then grasp . . .'

There is a poem of Thomas Hardy's, 'One We Knew' written about *his* grandmother, of about the same date, which describes the kind of scene:

'With cap-framed face and long gaze into the embers,
We seated around her knees—
She would dwell on such dead themes, not as one who
                                            remembers,
But rather as one who sees . . .'

Standing on the southernmost tip of Portland (The Bill) on a day in early February 1969, with light sleet and snow showers soon giving way to clear blue skies, and deep blue sea—it was at first not easy to picture the scene of the turbulent wild seas and raging wind of that day in February one-hundred-and-sixty-four years ago when the great East Indiaman *The Earl of Abergavenny* went down. But looking from a point near the Trinity House lighthouse out to the east it was possible to discern 'The Race'—that mixture of two opposing currents which meet below the Bill in a south easterly direction—and which produce a rough choppy effect, even on a calm day. At first no shipping seemed visible, but as the eye grew accustomed, several could be picked out, of differing sizes and distances away. One was the lightship now marking the treacherous rocks, The Shambles, lying southeast of Portland at a distance of three miles. With a gale and mountainous seas such as John Wordsworth had to face, it seemed too far out from the land for the ship's guns to be heard.

The roar of the sea would be deafening, as it enters Cave Hole, the cavern under the cliffs, and lashes the rocks; and the howling wind would add to the noise, at that distance from the shore. Another twenty minutes, the faithful, friendly Gilpin had said, and safety would have been reached on Weymouth sands. Coming off the Isle of Portland and turning inland, the whole extent of Chesil Beach lies below on the left, a clear golden strip with the innocent seeming blue sea—and inland water the other side of it. But on a rough day the sea roars as it surges back and rushes forward crashing the pebbles high on the steep bank, its shape unchanging,[2] the movement ever changing, as it hurls the glistening stones onto the bay that is called Deadman's, because drowned seamen were cast up here.

John Wordsworth's body was the last to be brought ashore; six weeks after the wreck, on March 21st, 1805 it was reported found. At first it was carried, most probably by the local fishermen, to the shelter of the ferryman's house, near the Fleet. C. H. Stewart, one of his officers came down and identified the drowned seaman as John Wordsworth, the missing Commander of *The Abergavenny*. Word would then be sent up to Belfield House, at nearby Wyke, the home of Mrs. Buxton. We are informed of this in a letter from Mr. Stewart to Captain Wordsworth, of Penrith; he speaks of having identified the body on March 21st, and then gives details of the funeral: 'Interred at Wyke, near Weymouth— respectfully attended by twelve members [of the ship], and Captain Connor, Captain Ingram, R.N., Mr. Weston, late Mayor of Weymouth—the principal mourners. The funeral was, by particular desire, under the direction of Mrs. Buxton,[3] a distant relation of Mrs. C. Wordsworth . . .'

Belfield house is described as: 'The beautiful seat of Mrs. Buxton, called Belfield; it stands on a rising ground, commanding a most extensive prospect of the channel, the Isle of Portland, and the Dorsetshire coast, as far as St. Alban's Head, as well as a very picturesque home view . . .' It was built between 1775 and 1780 by Mr. Isaac Buxton, a London Merchant, and was used by his widow (Fanny Burney's Mrs. B.) as a summer retreat for the rest of her life. It is in the Parish of Wyke Regis, and is a finely proportioned Palladian mansion, with a portico, its park now carved up into separate building plots for modern villas. It would have been a near and most convenient house for John's body to have rested, the night before the funeral at Wyke Church.

9. The Characters in the Novels

Directly opposite notions . . . spirit
and gentleness being incompatible.

JANE AUSTEN, *Persuasion.*

'It fell to Anne's lot to be placed rather apart with Captain
Benwick; and a very good impulse of her nature obliged her
to begin an acquaintance with him. He was shy, and disposed
to abstraction; but the engaging mildness of her countenance,
and gentleness of her manners, soon had their effect; and
Anne was well repaid the first trouble of exertion.[1] He was
evidently a young man of considerable taste in reading,
though principally in poetry; and besides the persuasion of
having given him at least an evening's indulgence in the discussion of subjects, which his usual companions probably had
no concern in, she had the hope of being of real use to him in
some suggestions as to the duty and benefit of struggling
against affliction, which had naturally grown out of their
conversation. For, though shy, he did not seem reserved; it
had rather the appearance of feelings glad to burst their usual
restraints; and having talked of poetry, the richness of the
present age, and gone through a brief comparison of opinion
as to the first rate poets, trying to ascertain whether 'Mar-
mion' or 'The Lady of the Lake' were to be preferred, and how
ranked 'The Giaour' and 'Bride of Abydos'; and moreover,
how 'The Giaour' was to be pronounced, he showed himself
so intimately acquainted with all the tenderest songs of the
one poet, and all the impassioned descriptions of hopeless

agony of the other; he repeated, with such tremulous feeling, the various lines which imaged a broken heart, or a mind destroyed by wretchedness, and looked so entirely as if he meant to be understood, that she ventured to hope he did not always read only poetry; and to say, that she thought it was the misfortune of poetry, to be seldom safely enjoyed by those who enjoy it completely; and that the strong feelings which alone could estimate it truly, were the very feelings which ought to taste it but sparingly.

'His looks showing him not pained but pleased with this allusion to his situation, she was emboldened to go on; and feeling in herself the right of seniority of mind, she ventured to recommend a larger allowance of prose in his daily study; and on being requested to particularise, mentioned such works of our best moralists, such collections of the finest letters, such memoirs of characters of worth and suffering, as occurred to her at the moment as calculated to rouse and fortify the mind by the highest precepts, and the strongest examples of moral and religious endurances.

'Captain Benwick listened attentively, and seemed grateful for the interest implied; and though with a shake of the head, and sighs which declared his little faith in the efficacy of any books on grief like his, noted down the names of those she recommended, and promised to procure them.'

The character of Captain Benwick is of great interest in the context of the identification of the hero of Jane Austen's West Country romance. If we look closely at the description of him in *Persuasion*, it is probable that we shall see that he is a composite creation, and if analysed he is found to contain more than one person who may be identifiable in real life.

The passage describing Anne Elliot's successful efforts to rouse and to help Captain Benwick quoted above, can be thought of as describing John Wordsworth, at least in those phrases where he is described as 'shy', and 'though shy, he did not seem reserved; it had rather the appearance of feelings glad to burst their usual restraints'. We have seen, how in a letter dated March 16th, 1805, William Wordsworth describes his brother John: 'Our brother was so modest and shy a man, that not one tenth part of his worth, above all his taste, genius and intellectual merits, was known to anybody but ourselves and Coleridge . . . my father in allusion to this part of his disposition used to call him Ibex, the shyest of all the beasts.'

Then, in the same letter, William goes on: 'John, as a sailor being accustomed to live with men with whom he had little sympathy and who did not value or understand what he valued and having been from his earliest infancy of most lonely and retired habits with all the deepest parts of his nature shut up within himself.' This latter description is surely echoed in the description of Captain Benwick: 'For though shy, he did not seem reserved; it had rather the appearance of feelings glad to burst their usual restraints'; and again: 'the persuasion of having given him at least an evening's indulgence in the discussion of subjects which his usual companions had probably no concern in.'

The passage quoted goes on: 'He showed himself so intimately acquainted with all the tenderest songs of the one poet [Scott], and all the impassioned descriptions of hopeless agony of the other [Byron], he repeated, with such tremulous feeling, the various lines which imaged a broken heart or a mind destroyed by wretchedness, and looked so entirely as if he meant to be understood, that she ventured to hope he did not always read only poetry.' These lines are very interesting. The picture of a young man, lodging with friends, withdrawn into himself through a deep grief and depression, caused by the loss of a beloved future wife, and then the heroine, a visitor, with other young people, chancing to be seated near him contrives to revive in him interest in life again by the depth of her sympathy and understanding, and intellectual powers.

When Jane Austen was just eighteen years of age, she appears to have been to a dance at the Assembly Rooms at Southampton; in December 1793, with her sister Cassandra and most probably other friends and members of her family. We do not know the reason for her visit to Southampton at that time. It is interesting to consider the possibility of another young visitor to the town in the autumn and winter of 1793 —William Wordsworth, the poet, then aged twenty-three. About his movements for these months there is, as Mrs. Moorman tells us 'a cloud of impenetrable mystery'. He had been trying to return to Paris. Some critics have said this was to see Annette Vallon, and their child. Of this we can know nothing. But William seems loth to join Dorothy at Halifax as he had promised, and whether he went to Paris that autumn or not, he may very well have hung about on the south coast hoping for news from incoming emigrés of one kind or another. So that it is very possible he may have been in Southampton during the time of Jane's visit there in December 1793. The chance of his going to the assembly rooms to pass the time (he was an enthusiastic dancer), is likely. The description which Captain Benwick gives in *Persuasion*: 'lines which imaged a broken heart, or a mind destroyed by wretchedness' do find an echo in Wordsworth's poem 'Vaudracor and Julia':

'Nor could the voice of Freedom which through France
Full speedily resounded, public hope,
Or personal memory of his own deep wrongs,
Rouse him: but in those solitary shades
His days he wasted, an imbecile mind!'

However, in spite of the fascinating possibility that Captain Benwick is in part composed of the two Wordsworth brothers, the one the handsome shy sailor, and silent poet, and the other the passionate poet whose imagination at this period is coloured with Gothic Romanticism, Benwick does remain a shadowy figure, almost more so than Jane Fairfax. We must feel his creator meant this to be so, and although in the end he marries the countryman's daughter, there is no doubt that Anne's seniority of mind diverted[2] him and helped to put him onto the road to that permanent healing which in real life Dorothy and later Mary, were so wonderfully to continue for William. That a woman as brilliant as Jane Austen would not have been a suitable partner for William we cannot doubt, and he, in his intuitive wisdom would know this too. He must always be the dominant personality in his household. That is why he chose Mary, his perfect mate. And John, the sanguine, witty, yet deeply unselfish, serious and sensitive mind, was the perfect partner for Jane. She was equally unselfish, serious and sensitive, and gloriously witty. It was an attraction of equals—like attracted to like.

When Louisa Musgrove falls on the pavement of the Cobb at Lyme, at the foot of the steps leading to the upper Cobb, she is apparently dead; the scene is described in Chapter 12 of *Persuasion*:

'There was too much wind to make the high part of the new Cobb pleasant for the ladies, and they agreed to get down the steps to the lower, and all were contented to pass quietly and carefully down the steep flight, excepting Louisa; she must be jumped down them by Captain Wentworth. In all their walks, he had had to jump her from the stiles; the sensation was delightful to her. The hardness of the pavement for her feet, made him less willing upon the present occasion; he did it, however; she was safely down, and instantly, to show her enjoyment, ran up the steps to be jumped down again. He advised her against it, thought the jar too great;

but no, he reasoned and talked in vain; she smiled and said, 'I am determined I will': he put out his hands; she was too precipitate by half a second, she fell on the pavement on the Lower Cobb, and was taken up lifeless!

'There was no wound, no blood, no visible bruise; but her eyes were closed; she breathed not, her face was like death. The horror of the moment to all who stood around!

'Captain Wentworth who had caught her up, knelt with her in his arms, looking on her with a face as pallid as her own, in an agony of silence . . .

' "Is there no one to help me?" were the first words which burst from Captain Wentworth; in a tone of despair, and as if all his own strength were gone.

' "Go to him go to him," cried Anne, "for heaven's sake go to him. I can support her [Henrietta had fainted] myself. Leave me, and go to him. Rub her hands, rub her temples; here are salts—take them take them."

'Captain Benwick obeyed, and Charles at the same moment, disengaging himself from his wife, they were both with him; . . . and everything was done that Anne had prompted, but in vain; while Captain Wentworth, staggering against the wall for his support, exclaimed in the bitterest agony:

' "Oh, God! her father and mother!"

' "A surgeon!" said Anne.

'He caught the word; it seemed to rouse him at once, and saying only "True, true, a surgeon this instant," was darting away, when Anne eagerly suggested, "Captain Benwick, would it not be better for Captain Benwick? He knows where a surgeon is to be found." '

Jane Austen has been criticised for making the character of the hero of *Persuasion* a man weak at the moment of crisis— blundering, unable to decide what to do for the best—until prompted by Anne, whose helpfulness and collectedness overcome his first stunned horror at the tragedy.

If we think of this disaster of Louisa Musgrove's apparent death as a tragedy, a tableau, representing in miniature the happenings on the larger stage of the real world, we may be getting close to Jane Austen's creative processes. She takes actual events, pours them into the crucible of her imagination, and rearranges them causing some events to diminish in scale and some to become greater, but never losing in the process her original intention—to try to understand the mystery of the personality of man and the puzzles and the paradoxes of his nature. And in this scene, the personality of one man in particular who was dear to her.

Compare the seeming weakness of Frederick Wentworth's stunned inaction when the first shock of Louisa's accident occurred, with the reports of John Wordsworth's behaviour at the time of his ship's disaster, when she struck on the dreaded Shambles.

Writing to Sir George Beaumont a month after the tragedy, William Wordsworth says:

'I will take this opportunity of saying that the newspaper[3] accounts of the loss of the ship are throughout grossly inaccurate. The chief facts I will state in a few words, from the deposition at the India House of one of the surviving officers . . .' (here follows T. Gilpin's memorandum—quoted above, Chapter 2). 'I have mentioned these things because the newspaper accounts were such as tended to throw discredit on my brother's conduct and personal firmness, stating that the ship had struck an hour and a half before guns were fired, and that, in the agony of the moment, the boats had been forgotten to be hoisted out. We knew well this could not be; but for the sake of the relatives of the persons lost it distressed us much that it should have been said. A few minutes before the ship went down, my brother was seen talking with the first mate, with apparent cheerfulness; and he was standing on the hen-coop, which is the point from which he could overlook the whole ship, the moment she went down, dying as he had lived, in the very place and point where his duty stationed him. I must beg your pardon for detaining you so long on this melancholy subject; and yet it is not altogether melancholy, for what nobler spectacle can be contemplated than that of a virtuous man with a serene countenance in such an overwhelming situation? I will here transcribe a passage which I met with the other day in a review; it is from Aristotle's *Synopsis of the Virtues and Vices.*

' "It is," says he, "the property of fortitude not to be easily terrified by the dread of things pertaining to death; to possess good confidence in things terrible, and presence of mind in dangers; rather to prefer to be put to death worthily, than to be preserved basely; and to be the cause of victory. Moreover, it is the property of fortitude to labour and endure, and to make valorous exertion an object of choice. Further, presence of mind, a well-disposed soul, confidence, and boldness are the attendants on fortitude; and besides these, industry and patience." Except in the circumstances of making "valorous exertion an object of choice" (if the philosopher alludes to general habits of character), my brother might have sat for this picture; but he was of a meek and retired nature, loving all quiet things. I remain, dear Sir George,

Your most affectionate friend,
W. Wordsworth.'

It must occur to readers of the Cobb scene in *Persuasion* that the momentary loss of balance and lack of presence of mind in Captain Wentworth at the moment of tragedy does jar; it does not seem to be the behaviour we have learnt to expect of him; from our knowledge of his character in the rest of the book, whether it is the firmness and wisdom with which he guided the early steps of Richard Musgrove, the unsatisfactory young son of the Musgroves, or the speed and endurance with which he broke the news of Fanny Harville's death to Captain Benwick, staying at his side to comfort him, and to lessen the shock thereby. Or the swift and calm manner with which he removes the troublesome two-year-old Walter from clinging on to Anne Elliot's back as she kneels at the bedside of the sick child, Charles Musgrove. This side of Captain Wentworth's character is more in agreement with William's assessment of his brother's character in his letter to Sir George Beaumont, except that 'he was of a meek and retired nature, loving all quiet things'.

What is it that the author of *Persuasion* is trying to do? There are, it seems, several alternatives. She may be attempting to show that an otherwise spirited and utterly reliable man may, in the face of a sudden shock, become, for a second only overwhelmed by it. Is she attempting to show that John Wordsworth may have been as momentarily off-balance as the newspaper accounts of the tragedy imply? Anne Elliot's immediate response to Captain Wentworth's cry for help may mirror an agonising regret in Jane Austen's heart that because Captain Wordsworth, like Wentworth, may not really have liked women on board ship (and because too of their long delayed marriage) she was unable to accompany him on his last voyage and be of swift help, as Anne was on the Cobb at Lyme. Jane may have seen the official reports of the disaster to the *Abergavenny*, as well as the newspaper reports referred to by William, and in her own mind fully agreed with the faith in his brother's conduct evinced by William in his letter to Sir George, but may she not have shown this so-called 'weaker' side of Captain Wentworth's nature in order to put forward the idea that a man of gentleness and imagination may at the same time be a man of spirit and courage? Something of this is conveyed very clearly in the conversation which Anne has with Admiral Croft as she walks home with him up Milsom Street, meeting him at a print-shop window,

where he is examining and criticising a very indifferent painting of a boat. He tells Anne he has 'something to tell her as
they go along'. After various delays, caused by meeting several
friends—the Admiral does at last get on to the subject—
which is the news of Louisa Musgrove's engagement to James
Benwick.

' "I thought Captain Benwick a very pleasing young man,"
said Anne, "and I understand that he bears an excellent
character."

' "Oh! yes, yes, there is not a word to be said against James
Benwick. He is only a commander, it is true, made last
summer, and these are bad times for getting on, but he has
not another fault that I know of. An excellent good-hearted
fellow, I assure you, a very active, zealous officer too, which
is more than you would think for, perhaps, for that soft sort
of manner does not do him justice.

' "Indeed you are mistaken there, sir. I should never augur
want of spirit from Captain Benwick's manners. I thought
them particularly pleasing, and I will answer for it they
would generally please.

' "Well, well, ladies are the best judges; but James Benwick
is rather too piano for me, and though very likely it is all our
partiality, Sophy and I cannot help thinking Frederick's
manners better than his. There is something about Frederick
more to our taste."

'Anne was caught. She had only meant to oppose the too-
common idea of spirit and gentleness being incompatible with
each other, not at all to represent Captain Benwick's manners
as the very best that could possibly be, and, after a little hesi-
tation, she was beginning to say, "I was not entering into
any comparison of the two friends," but the Admiral
interrupted her.'

So to the Admiral and Mrs. Croft, James Benwick is 'too
piano,' too gentle, ('of a meek and retired nature, loving all

quiet things') yet we find him going off the Cobb for a surgeon—'he was off for the town with the utmost rapidity' and
again 'Captain Benwick had been seen flying past the house'.

But Mary Musgrove calls him 'a very odd young man'.
'Charles undertook to give him some shooting . . . he made
a very awkward sort of excuse; "he never shot" and he had
"been quite misunderstood." ' (A letter from John Wordsworth to Dorothy from Forncett Rectory, dated November
11th, 1800, is interesting in this context. He speaks of Norfolk
'at this time looking naked and poor, and as I am no sportsman, it is a very uninteresting place to be at, at this time of
year'.)

' "Charles laughed again and said : 'Now Mary, you know
very well how it really was. It was all your doing (turning
to Anne.) 'He fancied that if he went with us, he should find
you close by; he fancied everybody to be living at Uppercross;
and when he discovered that Lady Russell lived three miles
off, his heart failed him, and he had not courage to come.
That is the fact, upon my honour. Mary knows it is.' 'His
head is full of some books that he is reading upon your
[Anne's] recommendation, and he wants to talk to you about
them; he has found out something or other in one of them
which he thinks—Oh! I cannot pretend to remember, but it
was something very fine . . .' Miss Elliot was spoken of in the
highest terms! Now Mary, I declare it was so, I heard it
myself . . . 'Elegance, sweetness, beauty—' Oh! there was no
end of Miss Elliot's charms." '

' "And I am sure," cried Mary warmly, "it was very little
to his credit, if he did. Miss Harville only died last June. Such
a heart is very little worth having; is it, Lady Russell? I am
sure you will agree with me."

' "I must see Captain Benwick before I decide," said Lady
Russell.

' "And that you are very likely to do very soon, I can tell

you, Ma'am," said Charles. "Though he had not nerves for coming away with us and setting off again to pay a formal visit here, he will make his way over to Kellynch one day by himself, you may depend on it. I told him of the church's being so well worth seeing, for as he has a taste for those sort of things, I thought that would be a good excuse, and he listened with all his understanding and soul; and I am sure from his manner that you will have him calling here soon. So I give you notice, Lady Russell."

' "Any acquaintance of Anne's will always be welcome to me," was Lady Russell's kind answer.

' "Oh! as to being Anne's acquaintance," said Mary, "I think he is rather my acquaintance, for I have been seeing him every day this last fortnight."

' "Well, as your joint acquaintance, then, I shall be very happy to see Captain Benwick."

' "You will not find anything very agreeable in him, I assure you, Ma'am. He is one of the dullest young men that ever lived. He has walked with me, sometimes, from one end of the sands to the other, without saying a word. He is not at all a well-bred young man. I am sure you will not like him."

' "There we differ, Mary," said Anne. "I think Lady Russell would like him. I think she would be so much pleased with his mind, that she would very soon see no deficiencies in his manners."

' "So do I, Anne," said Charles. "I am sure Lady Russell would like him. He is just Lady Russell's sort. Give him a book, and he will read all day long."

' . . . Lady Russell could not help laughing. "Upon my word," said she. "I should not have supposed that my opinion of any one could have admitted of such difference of conjecture, steady and matter of fact as I may call myself. I have a real curiosity to see the person who can give occasion to such directly opposite notions . . ."

'Directly opposite notions . . .' 'Spirit and gentleness being incompatible.' Does it not seem possible—when we consider the descriptions of Captain Wentworth—'a remarkably fine young man, with a great deal of intelligence, spirit and brilliancy . . .' and the descriptions of Captain Benwick's traits—'of a soft sort of manner,' 'He will sit poring over his books,' that these two friends are really the same person; they are both active, spirited when occasion demands, but also gentle, and tender-hearted, 'loving all quiet things'. They illustrate Anne's point of meaning 'to oppose the too-common idea, of spirit and gentleness being incompatible with each other.' In the novel they are two people—sometimes active, sometimes gentle. In real life they are one—John Wordsworth.

We must feel, then, that Jane Austen, when she creates a hero in Captain Wentworth who can 'stagger' against the Cobb wall from agonising shock at a moment of crisis does so because he has the depth of imagination and sensitive perception of 'a silent poet'—'loving all quiet things,' but who yet, though called to "a way of life unmeet"—was able to master his horror (the horror which made him cry out—'O Pilot! you have ruined me!' at the first grinding impact on the Shambles) and 'a few minutes before the ship went down my brother was seen talking with the first mate, with apparent cheerfulness, and he was standing on the hen-coop, which is the point from which he could overlook the whole ship, the moment she went down, dying as he had lived, in the very place and point where his duty stationed him.'

So then Jane Austen (Anne Elliot) makes her point—and proves that 'the too common idea of spirit and gentleness being incompatible' is mistaken.

The point is further strengthened and underlined throughout the novel in the development of Wentworth's character; from the early descriptions of him: 'a remarkably fine young

man, with a great deal of intelligence, spirit and brilliancy'
and his feelings when he and Anne Elliot meet again seven
years later. He says to the Musgrove girls that Anne is 'so
altered that he should not have known her again!' 'Frederick
Wentworth had used such words, or something like them,
but without an idea that they would be carried round to her.
He thought her wretchedly altered, and, in the first moment
of appeal, had spoken as he felt. He had not forgiven Anne
Elliot. She had used him ill; deserted and disappointed him;
and worse, she had shown a feebleness of character in doing
so, which his own decided, confident temper could not endure.
She had given him up to oblige others. It had been the effect
of over-persuasion. It had been weakness and timidity.'

Then again, Wentworth's conversation with Louisa Musgrove during the autumn walk to Winthrop on the subject
of Henrietta's really wanting to visit her cousins and her
fiancé, Charles Hayter during the walk, but giving way to
Mary Musgrove who did not wish to visit the farm, until
firmly persuaded by Louisa to keep to her original intention.
Wentworth says: 'Happy for her to have such a mind as
yours at hand! After the hints you gave just now, which did
but confirm my own observations, the last time I was in company with him, I need not affect to have no comprehension
of what is going on. I see that more than a mere dutiful
morning-visit to your aunt was in question; and woe betide
him, and her too, when it comes to things of consequence,
when they are placed in circumstances requiring fortitude and
strength of mind, if she have not resolution enough to resist
idle interference in such a trifle as this. Your sister is an
amiable creature; but yours is the character of decision and
firmness, I see. If you value her conduct or happiness, infuse
as much of your own spirit into her as you can. But this, no
doubt, you have been always doing. It is the worst evil of too
yielding and indecisive a character, that no influence over it

can be depended on. You are never sure of a good impression being durable. Everybody may sway it; let those who would be happy be firm.'

And then Wentworth's lamenting over the last ill-judged, ill-fated walk to the Cobb at Lyme on their way back to Uppercross after the accident.

' "Don't talk of it, don't talk of it," he cried. "Oh God! that I had not given way to her at the fatal moment! Had I done as I ought! But so eager and so resolute! Dear sweet Louisa!"'

'Anne wondered if it ever occurred to him now, to question the justness of his own previous opinion as to the universal felicity and advantage of firmness of character; and whether it might not strike him, that, like all other qualities of the mind, it should have its proportions and limits. She thought it could scarcely escape him to feel, that a persuadable temper might sometimes be as much in favour of happiness, as a very resolute character.'

The conversation with Anne after their final reconciliation at Bath shows how far, how very far, Wentworth has developed. He tells Anne: 'He persisted in having loved none but her. She had never been supplanted. He never even believed himself to see her equal. This much he was obliged to acknowledge—that he had been constant unconsciously, nay, unintentionally; that he had meant to forget her, and believed it to be done. He had imagined himself indifferent, when he had only been angry; and he had been unjust to her merits, because he had been a sufferer from them. Her character was now fixed on his mind as perfection itself; maintaining the loveliest medium of fortitude and gentleness; but he was obliged to acknowledge that only at Uppercross had he learnt to do her justice, and only at Lyme had he begun to understand himself.

'At Lyme he received lessons of more than one sort. The

passing admiration of Mr. Elliot at least roused him, and the scenes on the Cobb and at Captain Harville's, had fixed her superiority.

'In his preceding attempts to attach himself to Louisa Musgrove (the attempts of angry pride), he protested that he had not cared, could not care for Louisa; though, till that day, till the leisure for reflection which followed it, he had not understood the perfect excellence of the mind with which Louisa's could so ill bear a comparison; or the perfect unrivalled hold it possessed over his own. There, he, had learnt to distinguish between the steadiness of principle and the obstinacy of self-will, between the darings of heedlessness and the resolution of a collected mind.'

There is a last minute record of Captain John Wordsworth's character, as it appeared to a Mr. Evans, and his family, passengers on *The Earl of Abergavenny* and who most providentially escaped drowning; in the short time of their acquaintance they became warmly attached to John. He is writing of John to William Wordsworth: 'It was the well-founded expectation of having a successful voyage, that he should in consequence be enabled to retire from the service and live with his family (as he fondly expressed himself), that animated every exertion. And in all his conduct, of which I was the witness, I only observed steadiness, judgement and ability, and in the serious hour of danger, firmness and resolution, which to the last he manfully maintained.

'It may be conceived that the mild and reflecting character of your brother was not so well calculated for the scenes he had to encounter as others who had less feeling, which imposes the appearance of more energy; but as far as I can judge he tempered his character with the qualities that rendered him equal to the arduous struggles of the profession he had adopted.'

There is another point which should be mentioned. After

the wreck of the *Abergavenny*, there was a rumour current in the City that John Wordsworth was drunk at the time of the disaster. This is entered into in some detail by Mary Lamb, who writes to Mrs. Clarkson, the Wordsworth's friend and wife of Thomas Clarkson, the abolitionist, and colleague of Wilberforce who was John's patron.

March 13th, 1806

'My dear Mrs. Clarkson,

Your kind letter would have given me great pleasure but for the concern I feel at the uneasiness you express at the unjust reports you have heard of John Wordsworth. It is upon your own account alone that I am distressed at it; for my own part I totally disbelieve it, and so does my brother and he desires me to tell you in the strongest terms I can think of, his full conviction that the injurious falsehood you have heard is utterly void of foundation. The report coming from an underwriter Charles says makes it easy to be accounted for, because it is a well-known fact that they always impute blame to the Captains whenever a ship is lost. My brother says that he never heard a whisper at the India House (or anywhere else) of poor John Wordsworth being drunk, which had that been the case would certainly he says have been known and talked of there. He is quite certain the India Directors were perfectly satisfied with his conduct, and that no blame has ever been imputed to him.

'We are very glad you have not told Wordsworth, and earnestly beg you never will tell him, because it may not be easy to get at evidence strong enough to make him perfectly satisfied. It was with great difficulty that my brother got at the intelligence he sent to Wordsworth, the survivors almost all being gone out to India in other ships. We think we can trace the story of his being drunk to this slight foundation. A gentleman of the name of Burgoyne, a cornet in the string, who was a passenger in the ship, told at the India House that a few minutes before the ship sunk, he had opened a bottle of Cordial, and persuaded Captain Wordsworth to take two glasses, and gave the remainder of the bottle to those who happened to stand near him, and that while he was in the act of opening another bottle to distribute more, the ship went down. This Burgoyne we endeavoured to find out. We were directed to him from an Army Agent to the Prince of Wales coffee house in Conduit Street. I went there, but he had left town, the Master of the coffee house promised to forward a letter to him from my brother. Charles requested Burgoyne to address his answer to William Wordsworth. I mentioned this circumstance to Dorothy but as she took no notice of it in her answer to my letter I am afraid he never wrote. I have been again this morning to this coffee house, to enquire for Burgoyne, and find he is now in Ireland. The Master of the house with whom I had a long conversation assured me that Burgoyne never imputed the least blame to Captain Wordsworth and that he never heard the least word of his being in liquor. You may place great confidence on this man's testimony because Burgoyne came to the Prince of Wales coffee house immediately on his arrival in town from Weymouth. My brother says that this bad report coming from an underwriter he is the less surprised at it, because it is a well-known fact that whenever a ship is lost the underwriters always blame the Captains, and he had no doubt, no more have I, that the story of Burgoyne's giving him the Cordial, was told from one to another, till at last two glasses became a bottle and then the underwriters said he was drunk. We do not even think it possible for any quantity of liquor to make a man drunk in the agony of feeling he must have been in at that time. But let me again beg you will not tell what you have heard to Wordsworth, because we are certain we can get no positive proof, without we see and talk ourselves with some of the survivors—and for that we must wait till they return from India . . .

'You say nothing of yourself . . . you do not even say how you are in health, but it must have been your anxiety about poor John Wordsworth made you forget what you must know we were so very anxious to hear. Will you be so kind as to write soon for I shall be uneasy till I hear if you are more satisfied about this injurious report. I wish you would feel as I do that it is most certainly *a wicked and malicious falsehood.*

'God bless you, my dear Mrs. Clarkson, my brother joins with me in friendly remembrances and affectionate wishes,

'Your affectionate friend,

M. Lamb.'

It is unlikely that William would have been at all difficult to convince of the truth of the Lamb's opinions about the rumour—and in this letter, with its tender concern for John Wordsworth's reputation, Mary Lamb does reveal how little they really understood Wordsworth's loving devotion to his lost brother—which went very deep with him; Professor Ketcham—in the introduction to *The Letters of John Wordsworth* (p. 3), says: 'The effects on Wordsworth of this prolonged and shattering grief have been traced repeatedly in his poems, in his philosophy, in the history of his creative imagination . . . Our question then, becomes a double one; Why was John's loss so deeply felt, and to what extent was William's praise of his brother justified?'

We must feel that the source of Wordsworth's grief—if it does indeed seem excessive—lies in his awareness of the fact that John had been on the brink of marriage. William's sensitive imagination would enable him to understand, to the full, Jane Austen's sufferings at John's sudden death. In his: 'Elegiac Verses, in Memory of my Brother, John Wordsworth, Commander of the E.I. Company's Ship, *The Earl of Aber-*

gavenny, in which he perished by calamitous shipwreck, February 6th, 1805', the poet says:

> '. . . He who had been our living John
> Was nothing but a name.
>
> . . . .
>
> That was indeed a parting! Oh,
> Glad I am, glad that it is past;
> For there were some, on whom it cast
> Unutterable woe . . .'

It would have cast such woe on Jane—and William may have exerted himself as he did to get at the detailed facts of the disaster for her sake. For he would compare her desolation and loss with his marriage and happy future with Mary.

In the process of working out the details of the accident at Lyme in *Persuasion*, Jane Austen chooses to use the word 'staggering' to describe Captain Wentworth's helplessness as he leans against the wall of the Cobb, for support. It seems an unlikely word to use, unless perhaps there is a hidden meaning in the choice, known only to the author. In Chapter 7 above, verses 23 and 24 from Psalm 107—(which Thomas Hardy puts into the mouth of the heroine of *The Trumpet Major* and the Major himself), have been quoted:

23—'They that go down to the sea in ships; that do business in great waters;

24 'These see the works of the Lord, and His wonders in the deep.'

Jane Austen, by an association of ideas, may well have had the following verses, 25–27, in her mind as she wrote her description of the scene on the Cobb at Lyme:

25 'For He commandeth, and raiseth the stormy wind, which lifteth up the waves thereof.

26 'They mount up to the heaven, they go down again to the depths: their soul is melted because of the trouble.

27 'They reel to and fro, and *stagger* like a drunken man: and are at their wit's end.'

Is Jane Austen defending John Wordsworth against his critics—those people, who, in the security of their own arm-chair position, gossiped and found fault with a man facing hazards unknown to them? Is she not setting the Psalmist's more compassionate and forgiving interpretation of a storm at sea before that of her contemporaries, with their censoriousness and too ready condemnation?[4]

10. The Naming of the Ship

It is requir'd you do awake your faith.

WILLIAM SHAKESPEARE,
A *Winter's Tale*, Act V, Sc. III.

In *Persuasion*, Captain Wentworth's ship *The Asp* was not among those in which Jane Austen's sailor brothers served. Usually she used the names of one or other of their ships—no doubt to give the 'right ring'. In a letter to her brother Frank, dated July 13th, 1813, she writes:

'I have something [Mansfield Park] in hand—which I hope, on the credit of *Pride and Prejudice* will sell well, tho' not half so entertaining. And bye the bye—shall you object to my mentioning *The Elephant* in it, and two or three other of your old ships? I have done it, but it shall not stay, to make you angry. They are only just mentioned.' So that in giving a fictitious name to the ship of the hero of *Persuasion* Jane Austen is departing from her usual custom. We may wonder at this, and perhaps feel that there is more than at first meets the eye in her choice of the name *Asp* for Captain Wentworth's ship.

Captain John Wordsworth's ship *The Earl of Abergavenny* took its name from the Neville family. Edward Neville (in the time of Edward III, 1392) a son of the Earl of Westmorland, inherited the estate of Abergavenny, and the title Earl of Abergavenny has been retained by his descendants. (The Wordsworth's were related to the Nevilles through their cousins the Robinsons.) If we look at a map, we can see that the town of Abergavenny is in a strategic position, on the borders of Wales. As the guide books say, it is an old town, beautifully situated on the edges of the hills, at the confluence (*aber*) of the Usk and the Gavenny, which is a mountain stream which rises at Blaen Gavenni, 1,249 feet up in the Bryn Aro mountain,—and flows rapidly down to join the Usk in the valley below at Abergavenny. The Romans, realising the importance of the site—built a fort here, the position of which is probably near the later castle. In the Middle Ages, Abergavenny became a stronghold of the Lords Marchers, being the key to the pass of Bwlch, north-west of the little town, up the mountainous valley of the Usk, into Wales. The whole of these valleys, of the Usk, and its small tributary the Gavenni, are of great natural beauty; but they were also the scene of much bitter fighting, between the Welsh and the invading armies of either Romans or Normans, and later, in mediaeval times, the English. Castles were built at strategic points and the passes over the mountains were vital, both for retreating armies, and invading forces. So much, then, for the name *Abergavenny*, with all its topographical, natural and historic significance.

The name *Asp* is, perhaps, more difficult. At first sight, it would seem to mean 'horned viper'—'the pretty worm of Nilus' as Cleopatra speaks of it, which seems to indicate tragedy in the mind of the author. It is possible that Jane Austen saw *Antony and Cleopatra* performed at Covent Garden during the second half of November 1813, while on a visit to Henry, at Henrietta St. London. There is a review of this production by Hazlitt, in the *Morning Chronicle* of 16th November, 1813.

But perhaps it may be possible to find another, additional, use of the word, which may help us to understand Jane Austen's choice of the name *Asp* for her hero's ship. In the notes left by Cassandra Austen as to the dates of her sister's composition of the novels, we can see that during the earlier part of the second period of her literary activity, the Peninsular War was being fought out in Spain between the invading French and the Spanish and their Allies. The names of the famous battles would ring in the ears of all the villagers throughout England, as the Mail Coaches[1] thundered by, Badajoz, Corunna, Albuera, Salamanca, Vittoria, Toulouse, and likewise the newspapers would be full of the details of these victories, and of the routes taken by the vanquished armies of Napoleon, as they straggled back in to France over the Pyrenees pursued by their conquerors, the Allied and Spanish armies. All this Jane would store up in her memory.

One of the best known of these routes back into France— La Vallée d'Aspe—bears a very close resemblance, in many ways, to the one we have been noting in Wales. There is the same rugged mountain scenery of great beauty. A mountain stream, The Gave (Old French—Gavenne) runs through it, the Gave d'Aspe. There too is the Roman pass over the Pyrenees, the Summus Portus, Le Port d'Aspre of the Song of Roland. The Aspe Valley, in the Western Pyrenees, extends from the Spanish border to Oloron in the French department of Basses Pyrenees, and is about thirty miles long. Gave (or Gavenne) d'Aspe and Abergavenny are too close both in meaning and spelling, to be dismissed as coincidence. We may feel that Jane Austen chose the name *Asp* for Captain Wentworth's ship, because for her, and for those few others who shared her sad secret, it masked the real name of her beloved's ship, *The Abergavenny.*

'Your first was the *Asp*, I remember; we will look for the *Asp*.' 'You will not find her there. Quite worn out and broken up.—*I was the last man who commanded her.*'

When Captain Wentworth says, 'I was the last man who commanded her,' Jane Austen is thinking of John Wordsworth, her drowned Commander. There are two brief but

127

vivid descriptions of the faces of beloved persons in the novels, who appear to be dying or dead. One is in *Sense and Sensibility*—Willoughby's description of Marianne's face the last time he saw her at the dreadful London party, as we have already noted: 'but not before I had seen Marianne's sweet face as white as death. That was the last, last look I ever had of her; the last manner in which she appeared to me. It was a horrid sight! Yet when I thought of her to-day as really dying, it was a kind of comfort to me to imagine that I knew exactly how she would appear to those, who saw her last in this world. She was before me, constantly before me, as I travelled, in the same look and hue.'

That could also be a description of John's face as it appeared to Jane at their final parting before he sailed—strained and anxious, white with grief. Whether she actually travelled down to Belfield House, Weymouth to view John's body after he was found we cannot know for certain. Dorothy Wordsworth tells us, in a letter to Lady Beaumont from Grasmere to Grosvenor Square, London, dated March 28th, 1805: 'Yesterday's post brought us a letter from my eldest brother in which he informs us that the Body of our dearest John had been found by dragging, and was buried at Wyke, Weymouth . . .'

We do know, from Jane's letters to Cassandra at the time of her brother Edward's loss of his wife, Elizabeth, that it was the usual custom for the nearest relatives to view the corpse of their departed dear ones.[2] The letter, dated October 15th, 1808, says: 'Edward's loss is terrible, and must be felt as such, and these are too early days indeed to think of moderation in grief, either in him or his afflicted daughter, but soon we may hope that our dear Fanny's sense of duty to that beloved father will rouse her exertion. For his sake, and as the most acceptable proof of love to the spirit of her departed mother, she will try to be tranquil and resigned . . . I suppose you see the corpse? How does it appear? . . . [the day before the funeral] I see your mournful party in my mind's eye under every varying circumstance of the day; and in the evening especially figure to myself its sad gloom: the efforts to talk, the frequent summons to melancholy orders and cares, and poor Edward, restless in misery, going from one room to the other, and perhaps not seldom upstairs to see all that remains of his Elizabeth . . .'

The second description of the face of a beloved person who appears to be dead is that of Louisa Musgrove lying senseless on the Cobb at Lyme: 'There was no wound, no blood, no visible bruise; but her eyes were closed, she breathed not, her face was like death.'

Wordsworth describes the finding of his brother John's body—in the sixth stanza of his poem 'To the Daisy':

> 'Six weeks beneath the moving sea
> He lay in slumber quietly,
> Unforc'd by wind or wave
> To quit the ship for which he died,
> (All claims of duty satisfied)
> And then they found him at her side,
> And bore him to the grave . . .'

Unscarred and unbruised by the buffets of the sea, sheltered against the wrecked ship, the face would be as described in *Persuasion*—'There was no wound, no blood, no visible bruise.'

So Jane Austen for her mother and sister's sake tried to reach a 'moderation in grief' and to become tranquil and resigned. Some of the paintings of Leonardo da Vinci seem to show forth this quality, perhaps especially La Gioconda—with the deeply sorrowing eyes within the cheerful-seeming face.[3]

In *Persuasion*, as in the last plays of Shakespeare, (and especially *The Winter's Tale*) there is the tragedy of earlier days, and then the characters seem almost passively to have things done to them until they are reconciled, brought together again by chance, until the final blessing of a complete restored relationship is won. Over all there is the beneficence of a growing awareness of nature in all her beauty—the description of the autumn countryside in the walk to Winthrop and the country around Lyme. A tenderness and a haunting beauty hangs about the whole novel which is not explicable on purely human terms; we are made sharers in a joy of a special kind.

In its first form, as we have seen in an earlier chapter, Jane Austen rejected the reconciliation scene; it was too close to real life and at the same time it is out of order. It is not in its true context with the rest of the story coming as a final scene instead of before the hero's latest voyage as in real life. So that in re-writing the reconciliation of Anne and Wentworth the author is carried onto another plain. She is now thinking of John Wordsworth as he would have been after the shipwreck feeling he has now entered fully into that joy—'sense-less joy'—he has become truly 'unshackled and free' of all those cramping conditions which fettered him in the 'way of life unmeet, for such a gentle soul and sweet'.

Compare Wentworth's eyes of 'glowing entreaty' with Leontes' description of Hermione's in Act 5. Sc. 1.—'Stars, stars, And all eyes else, dead coals—' So that, like *The Winter's Tale* with its joyful resurrection theme at the end— 'It is requirad you do awake your faith—' Anne and Wentworth—Jane and John—enter into their joy at the last.

'In the distance . . . an affectionate⁴ couple enter a delightful garden, like the fringe of the garden of the Hesperides . . . are the figures . . . to symbolise the hoped for freedom, perhaps not on earth, for the couple?'

11. Rambling About the Country

Rambling about the country on foot.

JANE AUSTEN, *Pride and Prejudice*.

There are one or two points in *Pride and Prejudice* which may seem to have some bearing on the identification of John Wordsworth as Jane Austen's betrothed and to point to a possession of an intimate knowledge of the Wordsworths or at all events to a similarity of tastes. One is the incident of Miss Bingley's horror and disgust at Elizabeth Bennet's walk from Longbourn to Netherfield: 'The distance is nothing when one has a motive; only three miles. I shall be back by dinner.' . . . 'Elizabeth continued her walk alone, crossing field after field at a quick pace, jumping over stiles and springing over puddles with impatient activity, and finding herself at last within view of the house, with weary ankles, dirty stockings, and a face glowing with the warmth of exercise.

'She was shown into the breakfast parlour, where all but Jane were assembled, and where her appearance created a great deal of surprise. That she should have walked three miles so early in the day, in such dirty weather, and by herself was almost incredible to Mrs. Hurst and Miss Bingley; and Elizabeth was convinced that they held her in contempt for it . . . when dinner was over she returned directly to Jane, and Miss Bingley began abusing her as soon as she was out of the room. Her manners were pronounced to be very bad indeed, a mixture of pride and impertinence; she had no conversation, no style, no taste, no beauty. Mrs. Hurst thought the same, and added:

' "She has nothing, in short, to recommend her, but being an excellent walker. I shall never forget her appearance this morning. She really looked almost wild."

' "She, did indeed, Louisa. I could hardly keep my countenance. Very nonsensical to come at all! Why must she be scampering about the country, because her sister had a cold? her hair, so untidy, so blowsy!"

' "Yes, and her petticoat; I hope you saw her petticoat, six inches deep in mud, I am absolutely certain; and the gown which had been let down to hide it not doing its office . . ."

' "To walk three miles, or four miles, or five miles, or whatever it is, above her ankles in dirt, and alone, quite alone! What could she mean by it? It seems to me to show an abominable sort of conceited independence, a most country-town indifference to decorum." '

Compare these passages describing Elizabeth Bennet's behaviour, with Dorothy Wordsworth's spirited reply to her Aunt Crackanthorpe's letter of censure, when Dorothy has been staying with her brother near Keswick:

> 'Windy Brow,
> near Keswick.
> April 21st, 1794.

'My dear Aunt,

'I should have answered your letter immediately—after the receipt of it if I had not been upon the point of setting forward to Mrs. Spedding's, of Armathwaite where I have been spending three days. I am much obliged to you for the frankness with which you have expressed your sentiments upon my conduct and am at the same time extremely sorry that you should think it so severely to be condemned . . .

'I cannot pass unnoticed that part of your letter in which

you speak of my "rambling about the country on foot." So far from considering this as a matter for condemnation, I rather thought it would have given my friends pleasure to hear that I had courage to make use of the strength with which nature has endowed me . . .'

From this letter, it is clear that Dorothy Wordsworth and Elizabeth Bennet (and her creator) are sisters in the deepest sense. The phrasing, the scarcely veiled wrath at the limitations of the narrow-minded older woman's criticisms—and the courage to speak her mind—give to Dorothy's behaviour a very close affinity with Elizabeth's. Compare too her replies to Lady Catherine De Bourgh's impertinent questions, when she calls unexpectedly at the Bennet's home, Longbourn.

Another character in *Pride and Prejudice* who may owe something to an intimate knowledge of William Wordsworth is that of George Wickham. The story of this young man's life, who, as an officer in a militia regiment, was stationed for the winter at Meryton, is strangely parallel in his early days, with that of Wordsworth—as seen through the eyes of his two uncles, William Cookson and Christopher Crackanthorpe Cookson, his mother's brothers.

Consider the account of Wickham, as told by Darcy to Elizabeth Bennet in a letter in which he gives her details of the young soldier's connection with the Darcy family:

'Mr. Wickham is the son of a very respectable man who had for many years the management of all the Pemberley estates; and whose good conduct in the discharge of his trust, naturally inclined my father to be of service to him, and on George Wickham, who was his god-son, his kindness was therefore liberally bestowed. My father supported him at school, and afterwards at Cambridge . . . My father was not only fond of this young man's society, whose manners were always engaging; he had also the highest opinion of him, and hoping the church would be his profession, intended to provide for him in it. As for myself, it is many, many years since I first began to think of him in a very different manner . . . My excellent father died about five years ago; and his attachment to Mr. Wickham was to the last so steady, that in his will he particularly recommended it to me, to promote his advancement in the best manner that his profession might allow, and if he took orders, desired that a valuable family living might be his as soon as it became vacant. There was also a legacy of £1,000. His own father did not long survive mine, and within half a year from these events Mr. Wickham wrote to inform me that, having finally resolved against taking orders, he hoped I should not think it unreasonable for him to expect some more immediate pecuniary advantage, in lieu of the preferment, by which he could be benefitted. He had some intention, he added, of studying the law, and I must be aware that the interest of £1,000 would be a very insufficient support therein. I rather wished, than believed him to be sincere; but at any rate, I knew Mr. Wickham ought not to be a clergyman. The business was therefore soon settled. He resigned all claim to assistance in the church, were it possible that he could ever be in a situation to receive it, and accepted in return £3,000. All connection between us seemed now dissolved. I thought too ill of him to invite him to Pemberley, or admit his society in town. In town, I believe he chiefly lived, but his study of the law was a mere pretence; and being now free from all restraint, his life was a life of idleness and dissipation. For about three years I heard little of him; but on the decease of the incumbent of the living which had been designed for him, he applied to me again by letter for the presentation. His circumstances, he assured me, and I had no difficulty in believing it, were exceedingly bad. He had found the law a most unprofitable study, and was now absolutely resolved on being ordained, if I would present him to the living in question . . . You will hardly blame me for refusing to comply with this entreaty, or for resisting every repetition of it. His resentment was in proportion to the distress of his circumstances—and he was doubtless as violent in his abuse of me to others, as in his reproaches to myself. After this period, every appearance of acquaintance was dropped . . .'

Then follows a description of Wickham's attempts to seduce Georgiana, Darcy's fifteen-year-old sister, during her stay at Ramsgate with a governess, who proved to be a most unreliable guardian.

The points of similarity in the story of Wordsworth's early life are interesting—if we always bear in mind the unsympathetic attitude of his older relatives and their unloving vision which clouded the facts of the young poet's early struggle for freedom and independence to fulfil his great destiny. As Wickham's, so Wordsworth's father was the steward of a great estate—in his case the Lowther estates in Westmorland. Wordsworth went to Cambridge (in his case through his own brains), and was intended by his uncles for the church—though he wished to study law—an expensive training. A living (Harwich) was found for him, he declined it, not wishing to be ordained since he felt he was too young when first leaving Cambridge. At one time he wished to be a soldier. He leads a life of 'idleness' in London, but eventually decides to go abroad to perfect his knowledge of French. There the unhappy Annette affair occurs; he returns, in poverty, writes to his uncle for assistance in obtaining a living as after all he now wishes to go into the church. This Canon Cookson refuses to do, and furthermore will not see William or invite him to his house, Forncett Rectory, and will have nothing further to do with him.

Dorothy gives a hint of William's disgrace in a letter dated

July 1793 to her friend Jane Marshall, written from her Uncle's home at Forncett:

'If my brother makes an engagement which will take him out of England or confine him to one spot for any length of time, then he is determined to come and see me at Forncett, if it be for one day, though he has never received an invitation from my uncle and though he can have no possible inducement but the pleasure of seeing me. You must know that this favourite brother of mine happens to be no favourite with any of his near relations except his Brothers [John and Christopher] . . . by whom he is adored . . . I have not time or room to explain to you the foundation of the prejudices of my two uncles against my dear William; the subject is an unpleasant one for a letter, it will employ us more agreeably in conversation, then, though I must confess that he has been somewhat to blame, yet I think I shall prove to you that the excuse might have been found in his natural disposition.'

'I have been much disappointed that my uncle has not invited William to Forncett, but he is no favourite with him, alas! alas!'

Thus we can see the creative process at work in Jane Austen, from these and similar examples. She does not need to search about, for the raw material for building, constructing, the different characters in the novels lies ready to hand. By exercising her powers of minute observation she sees that one person can become several people, seen through the eyes of others, reflected, as it were, in a distorting mirror, as in the case of William becoming Wickham. And Wickham, Benwick, Darcy, can all be drawn from William Wordsworth, three facets of the same man. Wickham, the idler, Benwick, the 'Gothic' poetic recluse, Darcy, the proud, reserved aristocrat among men, not choosing to explain himself to those who do not understand him. She dovetails and shifts too, the time scale, the period in which people lived. For example, Mrs.

Musgrove and her 'large fat sighings' about which people have been so offended is *herself*, Jane Austen, looking at herself, perhaps too candidly, too cruelly as in later years she still grieves and mourns; contrasting her plumper, older form, with her youthful, slim shape of earlier days—as Anne's, sitting on the same sofa together. Jane would turn the full light of inner criticism onto herself in that way.

In *Mansfield Park* there are a number of clues to be found which point to a more personal knowledge of the Wordsworth brothers and sister. Fanny Price's upbringing itself is interesting. At first among the unsympathetic girl cousins of the Bertram family, and unpleasant hard-hearted aunt, Mrs. Norris—who is always extolling their superiority to Fanny. Then the rescue by their kind younger brother, Fanny's cousin, Edmund, who is destined to become a clergyman. He draws out and encourages Fanny's good qualities, and sees that she has books, and leisure to read them, so that her more scholarly mind is nourished:

'Kept back as she was by everybody else, his single support could not bring her forward, but his attentions were otherwise of the highest importance in assisting the improvement of her mind, and extending its pleasures. He knew her to be clever, to have a quick apprehension as well as good sense, and a fondness for reading, which, properly directed, must be an education in itself. Miss Lee taught her French, and heard her read her daily portion of History; but he recommended the books which charmed her leisure hours, he encouraged her taste, and corrected her judgement; he made reading useful by talking to her of what she read, and heightened its attraction by judicious praise. In return for such services she loved him better than anybody in the world except William; her heart was divided between the two.'

Her cousin Edmund tries too to protect Fanny from Mrs. Norris's harsh strictures, but he is not always entirely successful. Take the scene during the rehearsals of the play—during Sir Thomas Bertram's absence abroad. Fanny is asked to take the part of the Cottager's wife, though she has begged to be excused from taking any part in the performance. All the young people backed by Mrs. Norris, urge her to oblige them, except Edmund, who tells his aunt not to continue to press poor Fanny against her will.

' "Let her choose for herself as well as the rest of us. Her judgement may be quite as safely trusted. Do not urge her any more."

' "I am not going to urge her," replied Mrs. Norris sharply, "But I shall think her a very obstinate, ungrateful girl, if she does not do what her aunt and cousins wish her—very ungrateful indeed, considering who and what she is." '

All this can be paralleled by Dorothy Wordsworth's upbringing at her grandparent's house at Penrith, where her grandmother's harshness and disapproval, always holding up the Miss Custs as models, and notable young ladies whose virtues Dorothy cannot hope to attain remind us of Mrs. Norris and Fanny. The servants too are rude to the Wordsworth children—again reminding us of Mrs. Norris: 'The servants are everyone of them so insolent to us as makes the kitchen as well as the parlour quite insupportable. James has even gone so far as to tell us that we had nobody to depend on but my grandfather, for that our fortunes were very small, and my brothers can not even get a pair of shoes cleaned without James telling them they require as much waiting upon as any gentleman . . . We are found fault with every hour of the day both by the servants and my grandfather and grandmother, the former of whom never speaks to us but when he scolds, which is not seldom . . . I sit for whole hours without saying anything excepting that I have an old shirt to mend, then, my grandmother and I have to set our heads together and contrive the most notable way of doing it, which

I daresay in the end we always hit upon, but really the contrivance itself takes up more time than the shirt is worth, our only conversation is about work, work . . .'

Compare the passage in *Mansfield Park* where William Price, on a visit from his voyage, is describing his adventures to his uncle, Sir Thomas, and Mrs. Norris's attempts to interrupt him:

'William was often called upon by his uncle to be the talker. His recitals were amusing in themselves to Sir Thomas, but the chief object in seeking them, was to understand the reciter, to know the young man by his histories; and he listened to his clear, simple spirited details with full satisfaction—seeing in them, the proof of good principles, professional knowledge, energy, courage, and cheerfulness—everything that could deserve or promise well . . . with such means in his power he had a right to be listened to; and though Mrs. Norris could fidget about the room, and disturb everybody in quest of two needlefuls of thread or a second-hand shirt button in the midst of her nephew's account of a shipwreck or an engagement, everybody else was attentive.'[1]

Dorothy Wordsworth too is rescued by a kindly relative, who recognising her originality of mind, sees to it that she has some leisure for reading as Edmund did for Fanny. Dorothy's uncle, William Cookson, also became a priest. She writes:

'I am now writing by that uncle whom I so much love, he is a friend to whom I owe the greatest obligations, every day I like him better than I did before. I am now with him two hours every morning, from nine till eleven. I then read and write French and learn Arithmetic, when I am a good arithmetician I am to learn geography. I sit in his room where we have a fire. I am now writing beside him, he knows I am pinched for time when I write, so he told me I might do that instead of my French.'

It would not be wise to read too much evidence of John Wordsworth's identity as the unknown admirer of Jane Austen into the parts about the sea in *Mansfield Park*—there are her sailor brothers to provide her with plenty of information, in her own family. Though the description of *The Thrush* going out of harbour gives an impression of a similar kind to that of Wordsworth's in his poem 'To the Daisy'— about his brother's ship—one of keen admiration for the two ships by all who see them:

Mansfield Park: 'You lost a fine sight by not being here in the morning to see *The Thrush* go out of harbour. If ever there was a perfect beauty afloat, she is one; and there she lays at Spithead.' And the third stanza of the poem speaks of *The Earl of Abergavenny*:

> 'And full of hope day followed day
> While that stout ship at anchor lay
> Beside the shores of Wight;
> The May had then made all things green;
> And, floating there in pomp serene,
> That ship was goodly to be seen,
> his pride and his delight!

Again, this can perhaps be thought of as mere coincidence.

But consider the passages about William, Fanny's brother. Edmund is trying to discover why she is so very unhappy when she is first come to Mansfield Park. 'On pursuing the subject, he found that dear as all these brothers and sisters generally were, there was one among them who ran more in her thoughts than the rest. It was William whom she talked of most and wanted most to see. It was William the eldest, a year older than herself, her constant companion and friend.' William, who is to be a sailor—is invited to come and visit his sister—before he goes to sea. 'Their eager affection in meeting, their exquisite delight in being together, their hours of happy mirth, and moments of serious conference, may be imagined; as well as the sanguine views and spirits of the boy even to the last, and the misery of the girl when he left her. Luckily the visit happened in the Christmas holidays, when she could directly look for comfort to her cousin Edmund.'

Turning to Dorothy's early letters to her bosom friend, Jane Pollard, the similarity of situation is striking:

'Forncett Rectory,
June 1793.

'I often hear from my dear Brother William . . . Oh, Jane, the last time we were together he won my affection to a degree which I cannot describe; his attentions to me were such as the most insensible of mortals must have been touched with, there was no pleasure that he would not have given up with joy for half an hour's conversation with me. It was in winter (at Christmas) that he was last at Forncett, and every day as soon as we rose from dinner we used to pace the gravel walk in the garden till 6 o'clock when we received a summons (which was always unwelcome) to tea. Nothing but rain or snow prevented our taking this walk. Often have I gone out when the keenest north wind has been whistling amongst the trees over our heads. I have paced that walk in the garden which will always be dear to me from the remembrance of those long, long conversations I have had upon it supported by my brother's arm. Ah! Jane! I never thought of the cold when he was with me.'

Dorothy's hopes of a little cottage to be shared with her dear William—and where Jane Pollard will be a welcome guest, are contained in a letter of July 1793: 'If we could erect a little cottage and call it our own we should be the happiest of human beings. I see my brother fired with the idea of leading his sister to such a retreat as Fancy, ever ready at our call, hastens to assist us in painting; our parlour is in a moment furnished; our garden is adorned by magic; the roses and honeysuckles spring at our command, the wood behind the house lifts at once its head and furnishes us with winter's shelter, and a summer's noonday shade.' And here it is interesting to compare the conversation of William Price and his sister Fanny as they travel together towards their parents' home at Portsmouth—'The novelty of travelling, and the happiness of being with William, soon produced their natural effect on Fanny's spirits . . . of pleasant talk between the brother and sister there was no end . . . or speculations upon prize money which was to be generously distributed at home, with only the reservation of enough to make the little cottage comfortable, in which he and Fanny were to pass all their middle and later life together.'

Here there is the mingling of William and John Wordsworth into the character and circumstances of William Price. Compare the exquisite beauty of Fanny's love of nature, and above all the moon and starlit night sky, with John Wordsworth's as shown in Dorothy's letters to Jane Marshall, after John's death—dated March 1805: 'For he had so fine an eye . . . Many a time has he called me out in an evening to look at the moon or stars or a cloudy sky, or this vale in the quiet moonlight—but the stars and moon were his chief delight . . .' The passage in *Mansfield Park* echoes these descriptions of John's love of the night sky. Fanny spoke her feelings (to her cousin Edmund), ' "Here's harmony!" said she, "here's repose! Here's what may leave all painting and all music behind, and what poetry only can attempt to describe. Here's what may tranquillise every care, and lift the heart to rapture! When I look out on such a night as this, I feel as if there could be neither wickedness nor sorrow in the world; and there certainly would be less of both if the sublimity of Nature were more attended to, and people were carried more out of themselves by contemplating such a scene."

' "I like to hear your enthusiasm, Fanny. It is a lovely night, and they are much to be pitied who have not been taught to feel in some degree as you do—who have not at least been given a taste for nature in early life. They lose a great deal."

' "You taught me to think and feel on the subject, cousin."

' "I had a very apt scholar. There's Arcturus looking very bright."

' "Yes, and the Bear. I wish I could see Cassiopeia."

' "We must go out on the lawn for that. Should you be afraid?"

' "Not in the least. It is a great while since we have had any star-gazing." '

Thus, as Dorothy tells us, would John have spoken, when he called her out to look at the night sky at the cottage at Grasmere, during his long sojourn with her and William in 1800.

The room at Mansfield Park which had by custom grown to be thought of as Fanny's own, the East room, contained all her treasures—'the room was most dear to her, and she would not have changed its furniture for the handsomest in the house, though what had been originally plain, had suffered all the ill-usage of children—and its greatest elegancies and ornaments were a faded footstool of Julia's work, too ill-done for the drawing room, three transparencies, made in a rage for transparencies, for the three lower panes of one window, where Tintern Abbey held its station, between a cave in Italy, and a moonlit lake in Cumberland'.

Among all the many subjects there must have been to choose from, it is of interest that Tintern Abbey and a moonlit lake in Cumberland are cherished scenes. Also worth noting is Fanny's choice of reading: ' "You in the meantime will be taking a trip into China, I suppose; How does Lord Macartney go on?" ' This refers to the work by Lord

Macartney, British Ambassador to China, and reflects Jane Austen's interest in China, the country which John Wordsworth must often have spoken of to her, describing his voyages to and from China in the East India Company's Service.

Sanditon.

It is possible to find some similarities between the speculative growth of the sea-side town of Sanditon, in the last of Jane Austen's novels—with the expansion of Sandown (Sande-town), Isle of Wight. John Wilkes was the promoter of the project; he it was who discovered the advantages of the place as a resort, and the little town grew in the late 18th century and early 19th century, when David Garrick and various literary and political figures of the period, came to the Island as Wilkes's guests.

Mrs. Sanders, a descendant of Sir Francis Austen, told R. W. Chapman in 1925, that she possessed a copy of *Sanditon* made by Cassandra, Jane's sister. She added this: 'My father, the Rev'd Edward Austen, a son of one of Jane Austen's sailor brothers, had been told his aunt Jane intended to name her last novel (unfinished) *The Brothers*. Perhaps it is the development of the Parker brothers, Tom, Arthur and Sydney, in relation to each other, and the society of Sanditon which would have formed the theme of the book, with the growth of the tourist trade of the growing little resort as a secondary plot. The strokes which are used to draw the character of Arthur, for example, seem to be pure fun, and it is the same with the sisters, Diana and Susan. All three Arthur, Diana, and Susan, who live together, are clearly meant to be examples of *Le Malade Imaginaire*—one day Diana writes to her brother, Mr. Parker (Tom), that she is 'suffering under a severe attack of spasmodic bile'—and that the sea air would probably, in her present state, be the death of her—(and he therefore does not expect them at Sanditon that season)—and the next she has arrived and is 'posting over the Down after a house for this lady who she had never seen and who had never employed her!'[2]

Mr. Parker, the eldest brother, is the business man of the three—and together with Lady Denham, the chief resident—is promoting the growth of the little seaside project which is Sanditon. There is a fresh crisp urgency about the style of writing which is perhaps new. This passage describing Charlotte Heywood's impression of the place from her window—after her arrival at Sanditon, is a vivid example of these impressionist strokes:

'Charlotte, having received possession of her apartment, found amusement enough in standing at her ample Venetian window, and looking over the miscellaneous foreground of unfinished buildings, waving linen, and tops of houses, to the sea, dancing and sparkling in sunshine and freshness.'

There are too the romantic passages—which have a different quality still, and are not easy to define. Their atmosphere is like a page from a Turgenev novel—*The House of Gentlefolk*—or a painting by the French impressionist, Monet. Particularly is this so of the passage, where—'Charlotte, as soon as they entered the Enclosure, caught a glimpse over the pales of something white and womanish in the field on the other side . . .'

Sydney Parker is no doubt going to be the hero of the book. He comes to give a tone of youth and vigour to Sanditon—in his own gig or light carriage, he 'was about 7 or 8 and 20, very good-looking, with a decided air of ease and fashion, and a lively countenance'. Quite a different man from his brothers—yet perhaps he is to have an affinity with Arthur—who, but for the spoiling by his womenfolk—his two sisters, Susan and Diana Parker—would have been as handsome and adventurous as Sydney. But the characters are not sufficiently

K

developed—and we shall never know how it would have been with them all.

It is possible, however, to discern Jane Austen's intimate knowledge of the Wordsworth family from her conversations with John, in this unfinished tale. They are, perhaps, merest echoes, of one or other observable trait in the Wordsworth brothers. Richard, the lawyer brother, and Christopher, the shrewd administrator, may have provided a hint towards the creation of Mr. Tom Parker, the promoter of Sanditon. John Wordsworth, being in normal health himself, may possibly have made a little gentle, good-humoured fun of Dorothy's coddling of her brother William, the moment he seemed only slightly out of sorts. The scene of Arthur Parker's fireside toast making, with the final dab of butter, while his sisters are not looking—has an affinity with some of the descriptions of a similar occasion of William in De Quincey's *Recollections of the Lake Poets* . . . 'Dry toast required butter; butter required knives . . .'

The side of John Wordsworth which had to be uppermost when dealing with the fashionable world of the East India Company's trading, and the acceptance of invitations to dinner—'I met in the streets [of London] four different people who all gave me pressing invitations to dinner,' he wrote in 1800—reveals his charm and personality. John also, at this period, owned a gig—which he tells Dorothy about, in a letter to her in 1802: 'I have bought a horse and gig. I drive all about London. I can scarce tell you where I have been. Windsor is nothing to me in distance.'

Sydney Parker's creator may possibly have glanced at these sides of John Wordsworth's personality, when she was sketching him in—with so light a touch—as the hero of *Sanditon*.

'Sydney is here and there and everywhere. I wish we may get him to Sanditon. I should like to have you acquainted with him—And it would be a fine thing for the place!—

Such a young man as Sydney, with his neat equipage and fashionable air.'

And so—with a light shake of the kaleidoscope—the different members of the family are re-assembled to form fresh patterns—and are new created.

'I think it quite fair to note pecularities and weaknesses, but I desire to *create*, not to reproduce; besides, I am too proud of my gentlemen to admit that they are only Mr. A. or Colonel B.'³

12. Conclusion

> . . . the tide retires
> Its last faint murmur on the ear expires.
>
> WILLIAM WORDSWORTH,
> at the Isle of Wight, 1793.

Richard Woodhouse, his close friend, said of Keats: 'There is a great degree of reality about all that Keats writes: and there must be many allusions to particular circumstances, in his poems, which would add to their beauty and interest, if properly understood.' Perhaps the same may be said of Jane Austen's work. In this study, there has been an attempt to explore the novels, to try and discover something about the raw material upon which she worked. It is a two-way process, for by doing so, we come nearer to a fuller knowledge of the author's own life and creative processes.

As we have seen, Jane Austen herself told her close friend, Mrs. Barrett, that she thought too much of her gentlemen for them to be thought of as only Mr. A., or Col. B.—they were her creations, not simply people she had actually known taken straight from real life, but were far more subtly created. One 'real' person can present entirely different sides of his nature, and his personality to different people. To one he may respond by seeming a lively, gay person, to another quiet and reserved, to yet another friend, he may appear active and practical, and so forth. All these separate strands may come together in one person in actuality. We may here think of Elinor and Marianne Dashwood, the sister heroines of *Sense and*

Sensibility. There is a clever poem about them, most probably written by her nephew, James Edward Austen-Leigh, when a schoolboy :

'To Miss Jane Austen, the reputed author of
Sense and Sensibility a novel lately published.

On such subjects no wonder that she should write well,
In whom so united those qualities dwell;
Where "dear Sensibility," Sterne's darling maid,
With Sense so attemper'd is finely portray'd.
Fair Elinor's self in that Mind is exprest,
And the feelings of Marianne live in that Breast.
Oh then, gentle Lady! continue to write,
And the sense of your Readers t'amuse and delight.
                                        A friend.'[1]

It may be that Jane Austen's young nephew was right in assuming that Elinor and Marianne are drawn largely from her own character. But it is worth noting here that the Wordsworth circle may also have contributed something of Marianne's sensibility.[2] Annette Vallon's letters to William are 'all sensibility' as Legouis says, and 'the pathetic strain never relaxes'.

So Jane Austen, by her great gifts of perceptive, creative genius, could form her own separate men and women from these diverse strands from the ideas which these different qualities suggested to her mind. She may caricature a particular strand upon which she is concentrating her energies—to create a Mr. Collins, a Mr. Price, or a Lady Catherine De Bourgh; or, more sympathetically, she may love her creations into life, an Anne Elliot, a Fanny Price, or a Darcy.

The passages in the novels which seem to show an intimate knowledge of the Wordsworths, clearly imply that Jane Austen was completely familiar with the details of their lives, from John Wordsworth. It would be surprising if it were not so. He was to be her husband, and they must have had long conversations together—when they would have exchanged details of their families, and the different members of those families. Of proof of their intimacy, we have to think of the similarity of background—of the landowners, scholars, clergy, sailors and merchants who make up the different people in their immediate pedigrees. And of how likely it is that in the England of their day those layers might mingle. We have only to think of a few possibilities. For example—Henry Austen's wife, Eliza de Feuillide, *née* Hancock. Her father was connected with India and served in the East India Company, and she was a favourite cousin of Jane's. Then too there is a connection through the Weller family, a name in the Kent pedigree of the Austens, and a Captain Weller, of the Bengal Service—whose daughter, Rosina, married the Reverend Jeremiah Awdry, of Notton in Wiltshire and became the mother of Sir John Awdry. Sir John married, in 1795, Jane, a sister of Catherine and Alethea Bigg Wither, the Hampshire friends of the Austens. There are closer ties, perhaps with these Awdrys, and mutual friends and relations of the Wordsworths.

It may have been Belfield House, the home of Mrs. Buxton, Priscilla Wordsworth's relation, which was rented by the John Awdrys in 1814, when they were seeking a cure for their young daughter, Priscilla. She eventually died at Weymouth that same year, at the age of 15 years, and is buried in Wyke Regis church, the parish in which Belfield House stands. We know that the Awdry family rented St. Boniface House, Ventnor, Isle of Wight in the winter of 1810–1811, and were to have rented it again in the year the young girl died. Jane Austen tells us so in a letter to Martha Lloyd, dated September 2nd, 1814—written from Hans Place, Henry Austen's home in London. She has been visiting her friend, Mrs. Hill (formerly Catherine Bigg Wither, now married to Reverend

Doctor Hill, Southey's uncle on his mother's side) at Streat-
ham—an aunt of little Priscilla Awdry. Jane writes: 'She
[Mrs. Hill] told me that the Awdrys have taken that sweet
St. Bon[iface House] ... hoped be ... (?) Ventnor (two lines
missing, with the conclusion).'

Bonchurch, Ventnor, Isle of Wight, was early noted for the
treatment of tuberculosis; the air was considered ideal for the
control and cure of the disease.

That 'sweet' St. Boniface House at Ventnor, as we have
seen, was in a most retired and beautiful spot. An 18th
century writer says of it: 'A comfortable house, and lies at
the foot of a steep mountainous down, on a little level plain,
and looks towards some long regular slopes of rock, naturally
covered with coppices, and between which a few partial views
of the sea open to the house ... it is so retired, it might almost
be styled a hermitage; and at the same time it boasts of all
that Nature can bestow.' And down by the sea, on the low
cliffs adjoining the beach, there are soft green little plateaux
of grass—and daisies still grow there—the kind we call 'ox-
eye daisies'—with long stems and serrated leaves and flowers
which remain open at dusk. These must have been the kind
John saw and spoke of in his letter to Dorothy in 1801—
'. . . and the daisies, after sunset, are like little white stars
upon the dark green fields . . .' It is easy to feel that John
Wordsworth loved the Island with a special affection. He was
able to relax there, as nowhere else. We read, in her letters,
and in *Mansfield Park* particularly, the Island held a special
place too in Jane Austen's heart. Why was this?

We know that they both loved their native land above all
others. In a letter, written from Portsmouth on April 11th,
1801 to Mary Hutchinson, John writes: 'It is my belief that
for an Englishman no place is equal to England.' Jane writes,
in a letter to Alethea Bigg, on January 24th, 1817, from
Chawton: 'I hope your letters from abroad are satisfactory.

They would not be satisfactory to *me*, I confess, unless they breathed a strong spirit of regret for not being in England . . .' The Island may have been England in miniature, to them both. There is a spiritual 'feel' about their descriptions of it. John's—in almost the only 'poetic' letter of his to survive— says : 'I have been on shore this afternoon to stretch my legs upon the Isle of Wight—the evening primroses are beautiful —and the daisies, after sunset, are like little white stars upon the dark green fields . . . in many respects this place is most exceedingly interesting as a landscape. The rich woods and fine bay, the interest that one must always feel, from the ships, and life there is upon water—the noise of seamen in the evening heard at a distance, the boatmen and fishermen near the shore . . .' And Jane, in describing Fanny Price's walk on the ramparts at Portsmouth, as we have already noticed, gives just a hint of the Island's beauty :

'The day was uncommonly lovely. It was really March; but it was April in its mild air, brisk soft wind, and bright sun, occasionally clouded for a minute; and everything looked so beautiful under the influence of such a sky, the effects of the shadows pursuing each other, on the ships at Spithead and the Island beyond, with the ever-varying hues of the sea.'

In her letters too, Jane Austen conveys her deep love of the Island. She is writing to her sister who has been giving her news of a family party's first visit to the Isle of Wight.

'Your account of your visitor's good journey, voyage and satisfaction in everything gave me the greatest pleasure. They have nice weather for their introduction to the Island, and I hope with such a disposition to be pleased, their general enjoyment is as certain as it will be just. Anna's being interested in the embarkation shows taste that one values. Mary Jane's delight in the water is quite ridiculous . . . I do not at all regard Martha's disappointment in the Island; she will like it the better in the end. I cannot help thinking and re-thinking

Conclusion

of your going to the Island so heroically . . . and am in hopes,
as you make no complaint, tho' on the Water and at 4 in the
morning—that it has not been so cold with you.'

Wordsworth describes his brother John's happiness in the
Isle of Wight, in the lines he composed after his death:

> 'And full of hope day followed day
> While that stout ship at anchor lay
> Beside the shores of Wight;
> The May had then made all things green;
> And floating there, in pomp serene,
> That ship was goodly to be seen,
> His pride and his delight!
> Yet then, when called ashore, he sought
> The tender peace of rural thought:
> In more than happy mood
> To your abode, bright Daisy Flowers!
> He then would steal at leisure hours,
> And loved you glittering in your bowers,
> A starry multitude.'[3]

Their re-union on the island, the happiness and joy they
both experienced in being together, would have increased their
love of the place. John Wordsworth's stolen 'leisure hours'
may perhaps tell us of these meetings. Perhaps they would
meet at Osborne, the girlhood home of Margaret Blachford,
who, by her marriage to Lovelace Bigg Wither, in 1766,
became the mother of Alethea, Catherine and Jane, and their
brothers. Or perhaps these re-unions, infrequent and longed
for, took place at St. Boniface—'that sweet St. Boniface
House'. In February 1968—the site (the house long since
gone) had a strange, compelling beauty all its own; there was
still the old, worn tethering ring let into the stone wall that
skirts the desolate and forsaken garden. Where once were
shrubs and a planted approach—are now wild flowers—a

153

grassy plot, backed by a sheer rock surface, in a cleft a stream can be heard trickling downwards to run into a wild plot of the former garden—now overgrown with dank reeds, bog iris, nettles. Above overhang sapling timber, self-sown, wild and luxuriant. High above yellow gorse covers part of St. Boniface Down . . .

And in the lines of William's poem of 1793, we can re-capture the pleasure of his brother, John, and Jane—at the Island:

'How sweet to walk along the woody steep
When all the summer seas are charmed to sleep;
While on the distant sands the tide retires
Its last faint murmur on the ear expires.'

De Quincey's description of John Wordsworth's end—in 'Recollections of the Lake Poets'—although inaccurate as to place of burial, does, no doubt convey the unspoken wishes of Jane Austen, and almost certainly, John himself.

'Six weeks his body lay unrecovered; at the end of that time, it was found, and carried to the Isle of Wight, and buried in close neighbourhood to the quiet fields which he had so recently described in letters to his sister at Grasmere as a Paradise of English peace, to which his mind would be likely oftentimes to revert amidst the agitations of the sea.'

So John Wordsworth—the shy, silent poet, loving all quiet things—yet, at the same time, ardent, warm-hearted, and with 'a gladness that is seldom seen but in very young people'—has the distinction of having influenced the lives, and there-fore the work, of two of our greatest writers, William Words-worth, his brother the poet, and Jane Austen, the novelist.

When Jane's sister Cassandra, told a niece (when speaking of Jane's romance years afterwards), that 'she had herself so warm a regard for the young man that some years after her sister's death, she took a good deal of trouble to find out and see again his brother,' she did not give her niece any details of her interview with Wordsworth. It may be of interest here to quote again the story which this niece, Caroline Austen (James Austen's younger daughter), wrote down, to record the facts as she knew them. This version is a little more detailed than the one given in the *Memoir*: [4]

'All that I know is this. At Newtown, Aunt Cassandra was staying with us (the writer and her mother, Mrs. James Austen) when we made acquaintance with a certain Mr. H. E. of the Engineers. He was very pleasing and very good-looking. My Aunt was very much struck with him, and I was struck by her commendation; she so rarely admired strangers. Afterwards, at another time—I do not remember exactly when—she spoke of him as of one so unusually gifted with all that was agreeable, and said that he reminded her strongly of a gentleman whom they had met one summer when they were by the sea—I think she said in Devonshire; I don't think she named the place, and I am sure she did not say Lyme, for that I should have remembered—that he seemed greatly attracted by my Aunt Jane—I suppose it was an intercourse of some weeks—and that when they had to part (I imagine he was a visitor also, but his family might have lived near) he was urgent to know where they would be next summer, implying or perhaps saying that he should be there also, wherever it might be. I can only say that the impression left on Cassandra was that he had fallen in love with her sister, and was quite in earnest. Soon after they heard of his death. Mr. H. E. also died of a sudden illness soon after we had seen him at Newtown, and I suppose it was that coincidence of early death that led my Aunt to speak of him—the unknown—at all. I am sure she thought he was worthy of her sister, from the way in which she recalled his memory, and also that she did not doubt, either, that he would have been a successful suitor.'[5]

Newtown is in Hampshire, on the border, near Berkshire, and 1 mile north of Burghclere, and south of Newbury. It is there that the meeting described by Caroline Austen took place between Cassandra Austen and Henry Eldridge. Cassandra had been staying with Mary (Rev. James Austen's widow) and her family, daughter Caroline and son Edward—who was Curate of Newtown.

A meeting between Cassandra and William Wordsworth could have taken place in 1828. Her mother, Mrs George Austen, died in 1827, aged 88 years. Cassandra was thereafter free to travel to visit friends and relations, and to make long-deferred visits. There were cousins in Staffordshire, at Hamstall Ridware, where Edward Cooper, Cassandra's first cousin, was Rector. Also the family of her mother's aunt, Mary Hoskyns (née Leigh—see note on p. 172), living in Shropshire. Wm. Wordsworth's journeys south to visit *his* relations at Brinsop in Herefordshire, and Cassandra's visits north to the border and midland counties may have suggested some halfway meeting point which would suit them both.

Sara Hutchinson, writing to Edward Quillinan from Rydal Mount, on January 27th, 1828, says: 'Mr. Wordsworth is not yet returned. He left Brinsop last Tuesday...' Whichever date is the correct one for their meeting, it is safe to say that William would do his utmost to arrange it—knowing how much importance Cassandra would attach to her task of returning all John's letters to her sister[6]—and, maybe, a portrait miniature of John. 'He met with a clever young German artist at the Cape..."

A record of their encounter and of their conversation together would bring us closer, no doubt, to a fuller understanding of John and Jane's relationship. But perhaps it is as well we have not such a record, for we have instead, to search the writings of the two whose loss Cassandra and William mourned, and let them speak for themselves, as they do, direct to our hearts.

NOTES TO THE CHAPTERS

NOTES TO THE CHAPTERS

Chapter 1. Jane Austen
1 *Jane Austen's Letters*, ed. R. W. Chapman, 2nd ed., 1959. *Letters*, No. 99, 1. To Martha Lloyd.
2 *Jane Austen: Her Life and Letters*. W. and R. Austen-Leigh, 1913.
3 Ibidem.
4 See page 149.

Chapter 2. Romance
1 *Facts and Problems*, Chapman, 1949. Ch. 7, p. 98.

Chapter 3. Shipwreck
1 The Dove Cottage Papers.
2 *Letters of Charles and Mary Lamb*, ed. E. V. Lucas, 1935.
3 *Wm. Wordsworth: A biography. The Early Years*, Mary Moorman. Ch. 1, p. 9.

Chapter 4. Biographical Evidence in the Novels and Other Sources
1 Leigh House, near Chard, Somerset.
2 *Letters of John Wordsworth*, ed. by Prof. C. H. Ketcham. Cornell U.P. 1969. Introduction, p. 17 and 18.
3 *Jane Austen's Letters*, No. 69. To Cassandra. April 11th, 1811.
'I was tempted by a pretty coloured muslin, and bought 10yds. of it, on the chance of your liking it; but at the same time if it should not suit you, you must not think yourself obliged to take it; it is only 3/6 per yard, and I should not in the least mind keeping the whole. In texture it is just what we prefer, but it's resemblance to green cruels I must own is not great, for the pattern is a small red spot.' (One line cut

out here). Is this because, perhaps, Jane goes on to recall John's ability to choose muslins in the missing line?

Chapter 5. The Evidence—Emphasis on 'Persuasion'
1 Quoted in Chapman: Facts and Problems.
2 It is interesting here to read Professor Ketcham's speculation about John Wordsworth's contempt for the rich and 'great'. (See *John Wordsworth's Letters*, ed. C. H. Ketcham, 1969, Introduction, p. 60.) He says: 'It would be interesting to know its source: it is bitter and persistent enough to have originated in some personal slight or in some irrational focusing of a shy man's sense of grievance.'
3 Part of an unpublished letter from Wm. Wordsworth to Sara Hutchinson. Printed in *The Letters of Sara Hutchinson*, 1952, ed. by K. Coburn, by permission of Helen Darbishire.

> Rydal Mt., Oct. 4th, 1813.
>
> 'My dearest Sara,
>   Dorothy you know is at Kendal: but Mary and I received your letter last night which was forwarded to her by to-day's post. We long for your return which I shall be most happy to facilitate. (Then he suggests plans for meeting her half-way, she is at Stockton) . . . what I should like infinitely the worst would be that you should prolong your stay, and deprive us of your presence and company for I love you most tenderly. This is the anniversary of my wedding day and every year whether fraught with joy or sorrow has brought with it additional cause why I should thank God for my connection with your family—Mary joins with me in blessing you as we have blessed each other.'

This seems to show the simple, strong affection between the Wordsworth brothers- and sisters-in-law and Dorothy. As in the case of the Austens—marriage united sisters and brothers of each family.

4 *Letters of Sara Hutchinson*, No. 52, p. 151. 'William says "Let a wife drift towards you" and you will have a better chance of success . . .'

5 Perhaps to visit Mrs. Mary Lloyd-Baker—a daughter of William Sharp, and a niece of Granville Sharp, the abolitionist, of Yorks—and a possible connection of Anne Sharp, Jane's friend. She died at Dawlish in 1812.

Chapter 6. More Evidence in the Novels

1 *Five Eighteenth Century Comedies*, ed. Allardyce Nicholl, 1931, p. 15.
2 Compare the lines in Wordsworth's sonnet, 'Calais', August 15th, 1802:

> '. . . Far other show
> My youth here witnessed, in prouder times
> The senselessness of joy was then sublime!'

Is not Jane Austen using the word 'senseless' as Wordsworth does in this sonnet—meaning a joy that is beyond the senses—unforgettable, and pertaining to the realm of the spirit? See also Coleridge 'Dejection, An Ode'.

3 Dove Cottage Papers.
4 Compare also line 83 in Wordsworth's poem: 'When to the attractions of the busy world . . .' 'And an eye practised like a blind man's touch.' Also compare Mr. Knightley's proposal to Emma in Jane Austen's novel of that name.
5 *The Letters of Sara Hutchinson*, ed. K. Coburn. Introduction, p. 23. Extract from a notebook of Edward Quillinan, reveals that it was Wordsworth's habit, when at all irritated or disturbed, to 'twirl a chair about'. Perhaps it was a habit of John's too?

Chapter 7. The Evidence—Emphasis on 'Emma'

1 Sir Egerton Brydges: *Autobiography*, Vol. 2, p. 40.
2 The book was sold to Richard Crosby & Co., of 4 Stationer's Court, Ludgate Street, London, E.1. for £10.
3 See *Emma*. Penguin Ed., 1966. Edited by Ronald Blythe, notes, p. 468. 'Money'.
4 John Wordsworth lived at No. 9 Southampton Buildings, Holborn, but his business and correspondence were conducted

from Richard Wordsworth's Chambers, No. 11 Staple Inn.
See C. H. Ketcham: *The Letters of John Wordsworth*, p. 193,
note 4–14.

5 Other admirers of the Portsmouth scene were Edward, her
brother, Mr. and Mrs. James Austen, and Anna, her niece.

6 See *A Tour of the Isle of Wight*, T. Hookham and J. Hassell.
1790—a description of being shown the interior of Appuldurcombe House, by the housekeeper, bears a resemblance to
Mrs. Reynolds in *Pride and Prejudice* at Pemberley.

7 It is of interest that Jane Austen, writing from Godmersham
to Cassandra at Chawton (*Letters*, No. 84, p. 335, Sept.,
1813) says: 'I am now alone in the library, Mistress of all I
survey—at least I may say so and repeat the whole poem
if I like it, without offence to anybody . . .' This reference to
Cowper's poem 'Alexander Selkirk' shows that she had read
Wordsworth's Prefaces and Appendix to the *Lyrical Ballads*
of 1802. In his discussion of what he means by poetic diction,
he objects to the 4th stanza of the poem 'Alexander Selkirk':

> 'Religion! What treasure untold
> Resides in that heavenly word!
> More precious than silver and gold
> Or all that this earth can afford.
> But the sound of the church-going bell
> These vallies and rocks never heard,
> Ne'er sigh'd at the sound of a knell,
> Or smil'd when a sabbath appear'd . . .'

and says:

The first four lines are poorly expressed; some critics would
call the language prosaic; the fact is, it would be bad prose,
so bad, that it is scarcely worse in metre. The epithet, 'church-
going' applied to a bell, and that by so chaste a writer as
Cowper, is an instance of the strange abuses which Poets have
introduced into their language, readers take as matters of
course, if they do not single them out expressly as objects of
admiration. The two lines 'Ne'er sighed at the sound,' etc.,
are, in my opinion, an instance of the language of passion

wrested from its proper use, and, from the mere circumstances of the composition being in metre, applied upon an
occasion that does not justify such violent expressions . . .'

Jane Austen's witty comment shows she had understood
Wordsworth's objection to Cowper's bad poetry in the offend-
ing 4th stanza—and also that she was interested in Wordsworth's writings and opinions; it is surprising to find this
interest, unless her attention had been previously drawn to
his work.

8　From the novel *The Trumpet Major* by Thomas Hardy.

9　In a letter to Cassandra at Godmersham, from Castle Sq.,
Southampton (*Letter*, No. 66, Jan. 30th, 1809), Jane Austen
writes: 'A letter from Hamstall gives us the history of Sir
Thomas William's return—the Admiral, whoever he might
be, took a fancy to the *Neptune*, and having only a worn out
74 to offer in lieu of it, Sir Tho. declined such a command,
and is come home passenger. Lucky man! to have so fair an
opportunity of escape. I hope his wife allows herself to be
happy on the occasion, and does not give all her thoughts to
being nervous.' This mention of a sailor husband's homecoming in this letter to Cassandra, reveals something of Jane's
anxiety in similar circumstances. Compare Anne Elliot at
the end of *Persuasion*.

10　From an account in *The Gentleman's Magazine*, Vol. 2, 1804,
p. 963. 'Linois Squadron defeated by China Fleet.' See also
the painting, signed and dated 1804, by Robert Salmon, of
the East Indiaman *The Warley* at the Maritime Museum,
Greenwich. Reproduced as Plate 18 in the H.S.O. publication
Ship Portraits, in the National Maritime Museum.

11　*The Gentleman's Magazine*, Vol. 2, p. 873, speaks of the
great joy when the news of the defeat of Linois reached
Bombay—and of handsome subscriptions got together to
reward the Commanders—possibly these were presented at
a reception when the fleet reached India? A similar occasion
may have marked the China Fleet's homecoming; it is known
the Fleet Commanders were rewarded for their bravery (see
Prof. Ketcham, *John Wordsworth's Letters*. Introduction,

p. 40)—and some sort of reception in home waters may have been a possibility.

12 *The Diary of Elizabeth Ham*, edited by Eric Gillett, 1945. Ch. 10, p. 52.

13 *Before Victoria*, Muriel Jaeger, Penguin Books, 1967, and *A History of India*, Percival Spears, Pelican, 1965. Vol. 2, Ch. 10, p. 122-3.

14 D.C.P.

15 'A King's Portrait Concealed.' *Country Life*, Oct. 24th, 1968, by Alastair Stewart.

Chapter 8. The Evidence from Other Sources

1 D.C.P.

2 Compare: S. T. Coleridge, *Inquiring Spirit* (ed. Kathleen Coburn, 1951)—August 25th, 1802, No. 186—'What a sight it is to look down on such a Cataract! . . . the leaping up and plunging forward of that infinity of Pearls and glass Bulbs, the continual change of the matter, the perpetual sameness of the form—it is an awful Image and shadow of God and the world . . .'

3 Mrs. Buxton, of Belfield House, Weymouth, was the widow of Isaac Buxton, a London Merchant, of Coleman St., London, and Snaresbrook, Epping Forest, Essex. He built Belfield between 1775–1780, as a summer retreat. Mrs. Buxton was Sarah Fowell, daughter and heiress of Joseph Thomas Fowell, Esq., of Coleman St., a successful Russia Merchant. The Fowells came from Ugborough, Devon, and were said to have been there for many centuries. Mrs. Buxton (in charge of John Wordsworth's funeral), was mother-in-law to Anna Lloyd, who had married Mrs. Buxton's son, Thomas Fowell Buxton. Priscilla Lloyd (Mrs. Christopher Wordsworth), was a cousin of Anna Lloyd. See *Belfield and the Buxtons*, G. D. Squibb. Privately printed by Longman (Dorchester) Friary Press, 1954.

Chapter 9. The Characters in the Novels

1 Compare Anna Lefroy's description of Jane Austen (*Life and*

Letters), 'She was naturally shy and not given to talk much in company.' See also *Letters*, No. 49, p. 178-179, from Southhampton, to Cassandra at Godmersham: 'Our little visitor . . . is now talking away at my side and examining the Treasures of my writing-desk drawer; her name is Catherine [Foote] and her sister's Caroline. She is something like her brother—what is become of all the shyness in the World?'

2 See *Persuasion*: 'It was you, and not your sister I find that my brother had the pleasure of being acquainted with, when he was in this country . . .' and 'I was six weeks with Edward,' said he, 'and saw him happy. I could have no other pleasure. I deserved none. He enquired after you very particularly; asked even if you were personally altered, little suspecting that to my eye you could never alter.'

3 *The Gentleman's Magazine*, 1805. Pt. I, Earl of Abergavenny Indiaman lost, p. 174. (See also Prof. C. H. Ketcham, *The Letters of John Wordsworth*, Introduction and Notes).

4 An interesting comparison to be found in Jane Austen's letter to her brother Captain Francis Austen, H.M.S. *Elephant*, Baltic. (*Letters*, No. 81, p. 313, Chawton, July 3rd, 1813): 'We have had the pleasure of hearing of you lately through Mary, who sent us some particulars of yours of June 18th (I think) written off Rugen, and we enter into the delight of your having so good a Pilot. Why are you like Queen Elizabeth? Because you know how to chuse wise Ministers. Does not this prove you as great a Captain as she was a Queen? This may serve as a riddle for you to put forth among your officers, by way of increasing your proper consequence . . .' Also compare extracts from Frank Austen's notebook (1807)—in *Sailor Brothers*, Hubback. p. 192. He speaks of the Ascension Isle and St. Helena—'This island [St. Helena] being in the hands of the English East India Co., and used by it merely as a rendezvous for its homeward-bound fleets (where during time of war they are usually met at stated periods by some King's ship appointed to take them to England) has no trade but such as arises from the sale of those few articles of produce, consisting chiefly in poultry,

fruit and vegetables, which are beyond the consumption of its inhabitants, and a petty traffic carried on by a few shop-keepers, who purchase such articles of India and China goods, as individuals in the Company's ships may have to dispose of, which they retail to inhabitants and casual visitors at the island . . . A few acres of ground . . . will seldom fail to yield as much produce in the year as would purchase the fee-simple of an equal quantity in England, and this from the extravagant price which the wants of the homeward-bound India Ships (*Whose captains and passengers rolling in wealth, and accustomed to profusion, must have supplies cost what they may*) enable the Islanders to affix to every article they raise. To such an extent had this cause operated that a couple of acres of potatoes, or a garden of cabbages in a favourable season will provide a decent fortune for a daughter.'

Frank Austen then goes on to praise the conduct of the masters of various vessels belonging to the convoy—and especially warmly commends for their skill and attention and the cheerfulness and alacrity with which they 'repeatedly towed for many successive days some heavy sailing ships of the convoy, a service always disagreeable, and often danger-ous . . . are specially recommended to the notice of the East India Company'. Perhaps such praise from a Captain of a man of war was a useful means of advancement in the Service of the Company, and one which would be earnestly desired. It is typical of the justice and appreciativeness which was characteristic of Francis Austen that the masters of the very ships which most retarded the progress of the convoy comes in for his share of praise, perhaps even warmer than that given to the more successful officers. 'I cannot conclude with-out observing that the indefatigable attention of Capt. Hay of *The Retreat* in availing himself of every opportunity to get ahead, and his uncommon exertions in carrying a great press of sail both night and day, which the wretched sailing of his ship, when not in tow, rendered necessary, was highly meritorious, and I think it my duty to recommend him to the notice of the Court of Directors as an Officer deserving a better command.'

These extracts from Frank Austen's notebook provide a contrast in his outlook, now scathingly critical of the East India Company's Captains, and their encouragement of luxury trade, and now praising them and sympathising over the difficulties of commanding a worn out old ship. They probably represent the opinions of the average naval man of the day, envious of the opportunities the East India Company's Captains had of making a fortune, but also sympathetic to those men without influence put in charge of old and cumbersome ships. It is probable Frank was hasty in his criticism of John Wordsworth, who seemed to have influence, and was in a fair way to make a fortune. Frank may have condemned John's choice of a pilot at the last, and this may perhaps be the underlying meaning in Jane's letter. She may feel Frank was a little too censorious.

Chapter 10. The Naming of the Ship

1 De Quincey, *The English Mail Coach*—Going Down with Victory. (David Masson. Vol. 13.)

2 Compare also *Letters*, No. 41. Jane Austen to her brother, Capt. Frank Austen, H.M.S. *Leopard*, Portsmouth, from Green Park Buildings, Bath. Evening, January 22nd, 1805, announcing the death of their father, the Rev. George Austen: 'The serenity of the Corpse is most delightful! It preserves the sweet, benevolent smile which always distinguished him . . .' No doubt John also received a letter with this news. He and Frank were both at Portsmouth at this time. Compare also Wordsworth's letter to Southey, June 24th, 1835 telling him of Sara Hutchinson's death: 'I passed a wakeful night, more in joy than sorrow, with that blessed face before my eyes perpetually, as I lay in bed.'

3 Compare also Wordsworth's poem 'Mathew' published 1800.

> 'The sighs which Mathew heaved were sighs
> Of one tired out with fun and madness;

The tears which came to Mathew's eyes
Were tears of light, the dew of gladness.'

4   See above. Chapter 7, Note 15.

Chapter 11.   Rambling about the country
1   *The Letters of John Wordsworth*, ed. Prof. Ketcham. Intro-
    duction, p. 17. 'P.M. Mr. Wordsworth, 4th Officer who had
    charge of the Longboat to the camp at Musinburg Island
    provisions for the Army, return'd with an Account of
    the Boat being drove onshore in the Gale and beat to
    pieces.'
2   Perhaps there is a hint of Dorothy Wordsworth in Diana
    Parker. Dr. Andrew Bell (friend of the Wordsworths,
    Coleridge and Southey, founder of the Madras system of
    teaching) called Dorothy 'The Antelope'. See *The Letters of
    Sara Hutchinson*, ed. K. Coburn.
3   *Jane Austen: Facts and Problems*, R. W. Chapman, 1949.

Chapter 12.   Conclusion
1   *Jane Austen: A Critical Bibliography*, Chapman. 2nd ed.
    1955. p. 40.
2   *Wm. Wordsworth: The Early Years*, Mary Moorman. p. 180.
3   William's poem to his brother John: 'To the Daisy', com-
    posed 1805. He speaks of:

        '. . . And thou sweetflower shall sleep and wake
        Upon his senseless grave.'

    Wordsworth is here thinking of the small common daisy
    which shuts up its petals at night, not the ones John saw
    on the Isle of Wight? Note also the use again of the word
    'senseless'.
4   *Jane Austen: Her Life and Letters*, W. and R. Austen-Leigh.
    Ch. 6. Romance.
5   Cassandra would be careful not to mention Lyme to her
    niece, in later years, if it was the place, almost certainly,

where a meeting had occurred. The identity of 'a certain Mr. H.E. of the Engineers . . .' is given in an obituary notice in *The Gentleman's Magazine* for November, 1828. It reads: 'November 6th, 1828. At Worcester. Lieutenant Henry Thomas Edridge, Royal Engineers, second son of the late Rev. Dr. Edridge.'

The date of the young man's death in November 1828, underlines the possibility of 1827–28 as the date of Cassandra Austen's visit to Newtown. 'Mr. H.E. also died of a sudden illness after we had seen him at Newtown.' From the Cambridge records we learn that his father was the Reverend Dr. Charles Lucas Edridge, Rector of Shipdham, Norfolk, till his death in 1826. *He* married in 1793, Miss Cadell, daughter of Alderman Cadell, of Gt. Russell St., Bloomsbury, London. The spelling of the surname with an 'L' is not correct. There was no one in the Engineers at that period with the name *Eldridge*. But in the military records Henry Thomas Edridge is listed as a gentleman cadet in 1812, and his career in the Royal Engineers given up to his death in 1828. Miss Constance Hill in her book, *Jane Austen, Her Homes and Her Friends* (1901), refers to the young man Cassandra met as Mr. Henry Edridge. There is evidence that a fine portrait (see p. 172), which has recently come to light, may be of this young man. The likeness to the Wordsworths is striking. Permission for its reproduction, opposite p. 16, in this book has been kindly given by the owner.

6 She would also return letters which Dorothy may also have written to Jane. There are in the collection of *Early Letters of William and Dorothy Wordsworth* fragments of letters to an unknown correspondent, from Dorothy. These twelve fragments, dating from 1792–1798, are said to have been written to Mary Hutchinson. But some may have been to another friend. They contain some of Dorothy's best descriptions of places and the natural scene.

7 *Persuasion*, Chapter 23. Anne's conversation with Captain Harville at the White Hart, on the subject of the miniature painting of Capt. Benwick.

Notes

This portrait of a young man has been said by military experts to be of an officer in the uniform of the Royal Engineers of a date between 1812–1819. It was discovered in a house in Shropshire and was known to have been in the family for many years.

Cassandra Austen, Jane's sister, when staying with her sister-in-law, Mrs. James Austen, and niece Caroline, at Newtown (30 miles from where the portrait was), was introduced to a young officer of the Royal Engineers—a Mr. Henry Edridge—whom she afterwards stated resembled very closely her sister's unknown admirer. Mr. H.E. died soon after meeting Cassandra—at Worcester—which is not 20 miles from where the portrait was discovered. The former owner of the portrait was directly descended from Mrs. George Austen's aunt, Mary Leigh.

The eyes of the young man of this portrait, with their peculiar power and intensity, will remind readers of that passage in the cancelled chapter of *Persuasion*—'and he was looking at her with all the power and keenness which she believed no other eyes than his possessed.'

It is also interesting to note the points of similarity between the portrait and the tinted pencil drawing of William Wordsworth by Henry Edridge, A.R.A., the artist and friend of the poet. Both have aquiline noses. In both, the chin is marked by a dimple or cleft. The mouths are well-shaped and strongly marked at the corners. Both also have strongly defined vertical lines on the lower cheeks.

GENEALOGICAL TABLES

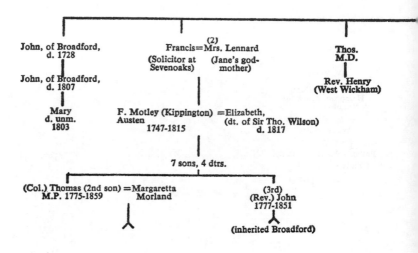

John, of Broadford,
d. 1728

John, of Broadford,
d. 1807

Mary
d. unm.
1803

(2)
Francis=Mrs. Lennard
(Solicitor at   (Jane's god-
Sevenoaks)   mother)

F. Motley (Kippington) =Elizabeth,
Austen   (dt. of Sir Tho. Wilson)
1747-1815   d. 1817

Thos.
M.D.

Rev. Henry
(West Wickham)

7 sons, 4 dtrs.

(Col.) Thomas (2nd son) =Margaretta
M.P. 1775-1859   Morland

(3rd)
(Rev.) John
1777-1851

(inherited Broadford)

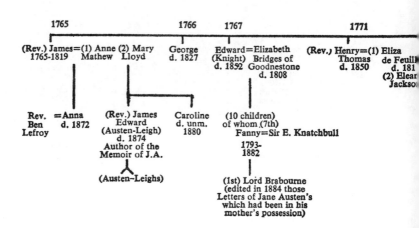

1765   1766   1767   1771

(Rev.) James=(1) Anne (2) Mary   George Edward=Elizabeth   (Rev.) Henry=(1) Eliza
1765-1819   Mathew   Lloyd   d. 1827 (Knight) Bridges of   Thomas   de Feuill
                                          d. 1852 Goodnestone   d. 1850   d. 181
                                                  d. 1808   (2) Elear
                                                                               Jackso

Rev. =Anna   (Rev.) James   Caroline (10 children)
Ben   d. 1872 Edward   d. unm.   of whom (7th)
Lefroy   (Austen-Leigh) 1880   Fanny=Sir E. Knatchbull
               d. 1874   1793-
               Author of the   1882
               Memoir of J.A.

(Austen-Leighs)

(1st) Lord Brabourne
(edited in 1884 those
Letters of Jane Austen's
which had been in his
mother's possession)

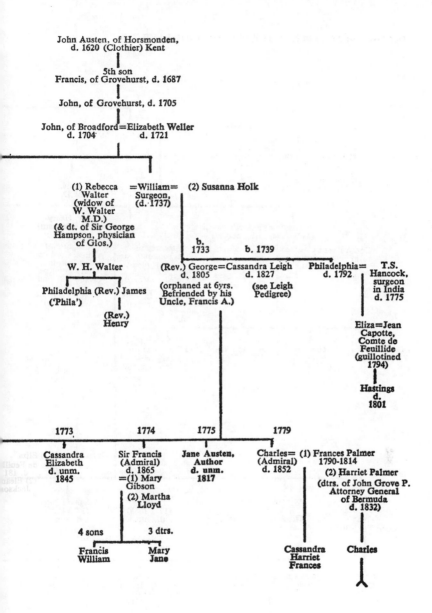

John Austen, of Horsmonden,
d. 1620 (Clothier) Kent

5th son
Francis, of Grovehurst, d. 1687

John, of Grovehurst, d. 1705

John, of Broadford=Elizabeth Weller
d. 1704   d. 1721

(1) Rebecca   =William=   (2) Susanna Holk
Walter   Surgeon,
(widow of   (d. 1737)
W. Walter
M.D.)
(& dt. of Sir George
Hampson, physician
of Glos.)

b.
1733   b. 1739

W. H. Walter   (Rev.) George=Cassandra Leigh   Philadelphia=   T.S.
                  d. 1805   d. 1827   d. 1792   Hancock,
Philadelphia (Rev.) James   (orphaned at 6yrs.   (see Leigh   surgeon
('Phila')   Befriended by his   Pedigree)   in India
                        Uncle, Francis A.)   d. 1775
        (Rev.)
        Henry   Eliza=Jean
                                                        Capotte,
                                                        Comte de
                                                        Feuillide
                                                        (guillotined
                                                        1794)

                                                        Hastings
                                                        d.
                                                        1801

1773   1774   1775   1779

Cassandra   Sir Francis   Jane Austen,   Charles= (1) Frances Palmer
Elizabeth   (Admiral)   Author   (Admiral)   1790-1814
d. unm.   d. 1865   d. unm.   d. 1852   (2) Harriet Palmer
1845   =(1) Mary   1817   (dtrs. of John Grove P.
             Gibson   Attorney General
             (2) Martha   of Bermuda
             Lloyd   d. 1832)

4 sons   3 dtrs.

Francis   Mary   Cassandra   Charles
William   Jane   Harriet
                                           Frances

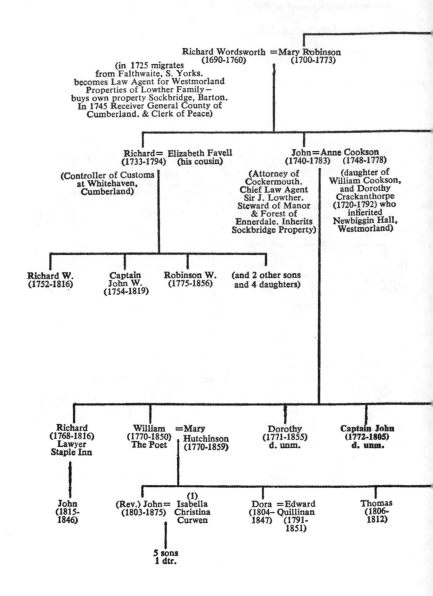

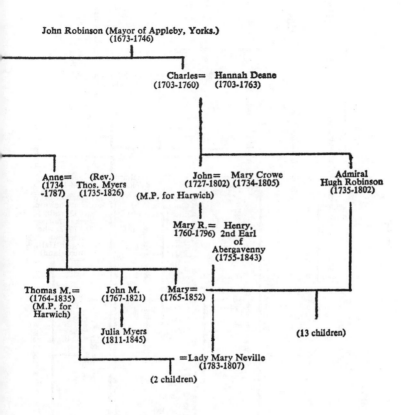

John Robinson (Mayor of Appleby, Yorks.)
(1673-1746)

Charles= Hannah Deane
(1703-1760) (1703-1763)

Anne= (Rev.)   John=   Mary Crowe   Admiral
(1734   Thos. Myers   (1727-1802) (1734-1805)   Hugh Robinson
-1787) (1735-1826)   (1735-1802)
        (M.P. for Harwich)

Mary R.= Henry,
1760-1796) 2nd Earl
of
Abergavenny
(1755-1843)

Thomas M.=   John M.   Mary=
(1764-1835) (1767-1821) (1765-1852)
(M.P. for
Harwich)

Julia Myers   (13 children)
(1811-1845)

=Lady Mary Neville
(1783-1807)

(2 children)

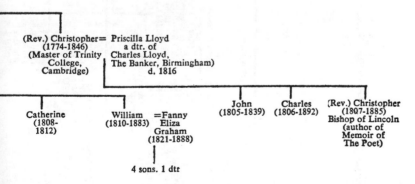

(Rev.) Christopher= Priscilla Lloyd
(1774-1846)   a dtr. of
(Master of Trinity   Charles Lloyd,
College,   The Banker, Birmingham)
Cambridge)   d. 1816

Catherine   William   =Fanny   John   Charles   (Rev.) Christopher
(1808-   (1810-1883) Eliza   (1805-1839) (1806-1892) (1807-1885)
1812)   Graham   Bishop of Lincoln
                          (1821-1888)   (author of
                                                                Memoir of
                                                                The Poet)

4 sons. 1 dtr

M

GENEALOGICAL TABLE OF THE LEIGH FAMILY

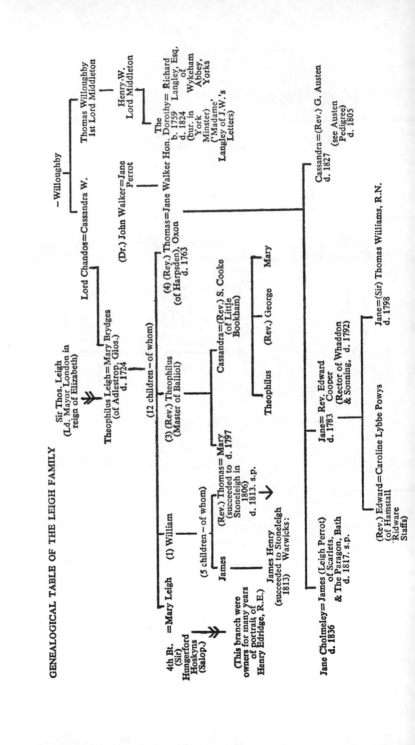

CHRONOLOGY

JANE AUSTEN

1775 Dec. 16	Jane Austen born at Steventon Rectory, Hants.
1793 Dec.	With her sister at Southampton. A Ball at the Rooms.
1795	*Elinor and Marianne* written.
1796 Aug.	In Cork Street, London (Henry Austen's home).
Sept.	With her brother Edward Austen and family at Rowling Kent.
Oct.	*First Impressions* begun. Finished August 1797.
1797 Nov.	With her mother and sister at the Leigh-Perrots' home, The Paragon, Bath (Mrs. Austen's brother James and his wife).
Nov.	*Sense and Sensibility* begun. *First Impressions* offered to the publisher Cadell, by her father. Not accepted. No letters survive for this year.
1797–8	*Northanger Abbey* (originally called *Susan*), written.
1798 Aug.–Oct.	Jane Austen with her mother and sister at her brother Edward's home at Godmersham, Kent.
1799 Feb.	At Ibthorp with Martha Lloyd.
May–June	With her mother at the Edward Austen's at 13 Queen Square, Bath.
Summer	At Godmersham with the Edward Austens.
Oct.–Nov.	Home at Steventon.
1800 Nov.	At Ibthorp.
1801 Feb.	With their friends, the Bigg-Withers, at Manydown, Hants.

	May	Jane Austen with her mother at Paragon, Bath.
	Summer	With her sister and parents at Sidmouth, South Devon.
1801	Autumn	The Austens leave Steventon, and settle at 4 Sydney Terrace, Bath.
1802	Summer	At Dawlish and Teignmouth with her parents and sister.
	Sept. Oct. Nov. and Dec.	With Cassandra at Steventon, Godmersham and Manydown. (Mrs. James Austen's Diary gives exact details):
	Sept. 1	Jane Austen and Cassandra reach Steventon Rectory.
	Sept. 3	They left for Kent.
	Oct. 28	They return to Steventon.
	Nov. 25	They left for Manydown (Harris Bigg-Wither proposed to Jane Austen).
	Dec. 3	They returned to Steventon.
	Dec. 4	They left for Bath. No letters survive for this year.
1803	Spring	*Susan* (*Northanger Abbey*) sold to Crosby for £10. Jane Austen at Ramsgate, Kent.
	Nov.	Jane Austen at Lyme. *The Watson's* written? (date of watermark). No letters survive.
1804		With Henry and his wife on a summer 'ramble'—(Weymouth mentioned).
	Sept.	With her parents at Lyme, Dorset. One letter survives.
1805	Jan. 21	Rev. George Austen died at 27 Green Park Buildings, Bath.
	April	With her mother at 25 Gay Street, Bath. *Lady Susan* written (from date of watermark on paper).
1809	April	Correspondence with Crosby about *Susan* (*Northanger Abbey*).

1811	Feb.	*Mansfield Park* begun (finished soon after June 1813).
	Nov.	*Sense and Sensibility* published by T. Egerton.
1813		*Pride and Prejudice* published by T. Egerton.
1814	Jan. 21	*Emma* begun (finished March 29th, 1815).
1814		*Mansfield Park* published by T. Egerton.
1815	Summer or Autumn	*Persuasion* begun (finished August 1816).
	Dec.	*Emma* published by John Murray.
1817	Jan. 27– Mar. 18	Composition of *Sanditon*.
	July 18	Jane Austen died. Buried in Winchester Cathedral.
1818		*Northanger Abbey* and *Persuasion* published by John Murray.

JOHN WORDSWORTH

1772	Dec. 4	Born at Cockermouth, Cumberland.
1790	Jan. 17–30	Midshipman John Wordsworth sailed on board his cousin's ship *The Earl of Abergavenny*—bound for Bombay and China on her maiden voyage.
1795	Feb.	On board the East Indiaman *Osterley* promoted to Fourth Mate.
	May	Sailed with combined fleets for Cape of Good Hope and the East.
1797	Feb. 8	Returned to England, and obtained new ship (Feb. 10th) *Duke of Montrose*.
	Mar. 1	Promotion to Second Mate approved. But mutiny broke out among crew. They said the ship not sea worthy. Sailed eventually from Portsmouth in July.
	July– Sept. 22	Detained for two months in Torbay, South Devon, owing to westerly winds. (Wm. and

D.W. had just moved from Racedown, Dorset to Alfoxton, N. Somerset.)
Resumed voyage Sept. 22nd.
No letters survive for period 1793–1800.

1799 Sept.–
Oct. 6
John Wordsworth arrived back in England. Went north to his Uncle Christopher at New-biggin Hall, near Penrith. At the end of October John joins William and Coleridge for a short walking tour with them. No trace of him from Nov. 1799 to January 1800. He probably returned to Newbiggin, but no record.

1800 Jan.–Sept.
Sept. 28
John Wordsworth at Dove Cottage, Grasmere. John Wordsworth returned to London in order to be sworn in as the new Captain of *The Earl of Abergavenny* in succession to his cousin, Captain John Wordsworth senior, then retiring.

1800 Oct. 4
Nov.
Letters survive from this date. Visit to his uncle, Canon Cookson and family at Forncett for two weeks. Also his brother, Christopher for a day, who is now a Fellow of Trinity College, Cambridge.

1801 Jan. 1
John Wordsworth accepted formally by the Court of Directors as the new captain of the *Abergavenny*, but did not sail till May. During this time, helped to see William's poems *Lyrical Ballads* second volume, through the press.

1802 Sept. 11
Returned to England. Wm. and D.W. in London on their return from France.

1803 May 3
early Sept.
Abergavenny sails down river from London. Reached China.

1804 Feb.
East India Co. China Fleet encounters a French Squadron under Admiral Linois in Straits of Malacca and defeats him.

Aug.	E.I. China Fleet arrives in English Channel. In the next weeks, John Wordsworth begins his campaign to obtain a more profitable voyage (see letters). Finally in October, he obtains the Bengal and China.
1805 Jan.	Letters from John as he leaves Portsmouth in *The Earl of Abergavenny*.
Feb. 5	*Abergavenny* wrecked off Portland.
Mar. 20	John Wordsworth's body recovered from the sea (six weeks later). Buried at Wyke Regis Church, Weymouth, Dorset.

ACKNOWLEDGMENTS

I should like to thank the Trustees of the Dove Cottage Library for allowing me to work on John Wordsworth's letters and papers connected with him; also Miss Nesta Clutterbuck, the Librarian, who made me so welcome and kindly answered some later queries. Professor C. H. Ketcham, whose edition of *The Letters of John Wordsworth*, was recently published by Cornell University Press, kindly offered his help. I have found his book a mine of helpful information. The Librarian at Weymouth allowed me to see his valuable collection of prints and paintings of Belfield House, and Mr. G. D. Squibb, Q.C. kindly gave me permission to quote from his book *Belfield and the Buxtons* published by the Friary Press (Longmans, Dorchester).

My thanks are also due to Mr. Jonathan Wordsworth for allowing me to quote from the Dove Cottage Papers; to the Cornell University Press for permission to quote from *The Letters of John Wordsworth* edited by Professor C. H. Ketcham; to the Clarendon Press for permission to quote from *Jane Austen's Literary Manuscripts* by B. C. Southam (1964), *Jane Austen: Facts and Problems* by R. W. Chapman (1948), *William Wordsworth: A Biography* by Mary Moorman (1957), *Jane Austen: A Critical Bibliography* by R. W. Chapman (2nd Edition, 1955), *The Letters of William and Dorothy Wordsworth* edited by Ernest de Selincourt revised by Mary Moorman (2nd ed., 1969); to the Oxford University Press for permission to quote from *Jane Austen's Letters to her sister Cassandra and others*, collected and edited by R. W. Chapman, (1952) and from *Five Eighteenth Century Comedies* edited by Allardyce Nicholl (World's Classics 1931); I have also used their editions of Jane Austen's novels and William Wordsworth's poems for reference and quotation purposes; to Chatto and Windus for permission to quote from Muriel

Jaeger's *Before Victoria*; to the Isle of Wight County Press for permission to quote from Alfred Noyes's 'Phantom Ship'; to Pan Books for the quotation from Miss Brigid Brophy's Introduction to *Pride and Prejudice*; to John Murray for permission to quote from *Personal Aspects of Jane Austen* of Mary Augusta Austen-Leigh (1920); and *The Life and Letters of Jane Austen* by W. & R. A. Austen-Leigh (Smith, Elder & Co., 1913); to Eric Gillett, the editor of *Elizabeth Ham by Herself 1783–1820* (Faber & Faber, 1945); to The Bodley Head for permission to quote from Jane Austen's *Sailor Brothers* by H. and E. Hubback (1906); to Routledge & Kegan Paul Ltd. for permission to quote from *The Letters of Sara Hutchinson* edited by Kathleen Coburn (1952) and *Inquiring Spirit*, Notebooks of S. T. Coleridge, edited by Kathleen Coburn (1951); to Penguin Books for permission to quote from their edition of *Emma*, from 'A note on Money' edited by Ronald Blythe, and from *A History of India* by Percival Spears; to MacMillan & Co. London, the MacMillan Co. of Canada, and the trustees of the Hardy estate for permission to quote from 'One we knew' and *The Trumpet Major* by Thomas Hardy; to Mr. Alastair Stewart for permission to quote from his article 'A King's Portrait Concealed' (Country Life, 1968); and to Dent & Sons Ltd. for the quotation from *Letters of Charles and Mary Lamb* edited by E. V. Lucas (1935).

I should like to thank Miss Pollard who has very kindly allowed me to reproduce her portrait of Mr. H. E. which was so romantically discovered in a woodshed! Also for allowing me to see a letter from Lt. Col. H. S. Francis, O.B.E. of the Museum of the Corps of Engineers in answer to her queries. My thanks are especially due to Miss Amy Howlett who has led me so graciously and kindly along the hitherto unknown path of publication. Lastly, I owe more than I can say, to my husband. He it was who taught me to study Jane Austen in depth, and later encouraged me to write about her.

C. P.

Index

A

Abbey School, Reading, 13
Abergavenny, Earl of (ship), 23,
  25, 26, 27, 28, 31, 32, 39, 45, 50,
  74, 77, 83, 84, 91, 98, 99, 100,
  101, 102, 103, 112, 119, 120, 122,
  127, 140
Abergavenny, Wales, 126
Abbey Mill Farm, 94
Adair, Robin, 59
Adlestrop, Glos., 12
Alfoxton, N. Somerset, 30, 35, 37
Allen, Mrs., 35, 36
Appuldurcombe House, I.o.W., 80,
  81
Asp (ship), 20, 21, 22, 32, 125,
  126, 127
Austen, Caroline (niece), 9, 16,
  155, 156
— Cassandra (sister), 9, 10, 13, 14–
  19, 37, 38, 45, 52, 53, 59, 76, 83,
  85, 89, 107, 126, 144, 154, 155,
  156, 157
— Edward (brother), 14, 52, 53, 59,
  128
— Mrs. (sister-in-law), 52, 53, 128
— Edward, Rev., 144
— Fanny (niece), 128
— Francis (great uncle), 12
— Frank (brother), 75, 76, 144
— Mrs. Frank (Mary Gibson), 76
— George, Rev. (father), 11, 12, 13,
  14, 19, 38, 62, 89
— Mrs. (mother, Cassandra Leigh),
  12, 13, 34, 38, 44, 52, 89, 92
— George (brother), 51, 52
— Henry (brother), 14, 37, 57, 59,
  67, 75, 85, 89, 90, 91, 93, 96, 126,
  149, 150
— Mrs. (Eliza de Feullide), 37, 57,
  59, 67, 75, 85, 89, 90, 91, 93, 149

— James, Rev. (brother), 9, 11,
  14, 52, 53
— Mrs. (Mary Lloyd), 52, 53, 155,
  156
— Rebecca (grandmother), 12
— William (grandfather), 12
— **Jane**, Life—*passim*
Novels
Emma, 56, 58, 59, 71, 86, 88, 89,
  93, 94
Mansfield Park, 36, 56, 76, 78,
  125, 137, 139, 140, 142, 151
Northanger Abbey, 35, 36, 56, 75
Persuasion, 20, 25, 32, 34, 37,
  38, 42, 44, 46, 66, 68, 71, 84,
  85, 104, 105, 108, 111, 112, 117,
  123, 125, 129
Pride and Prejudice, 55, 77, 96,
  125, 131, 133
Sanditon ('The Brothers'), 144–5
Sense and Sensibility, 56, 60, 128,
  149
Awdry, the, family, 80, 150, 153
Axminster, Devon, 30

B

Baring, Sir Francis, 90
Barrett, Mrs., 9, 18, 19, 148
Bates, Mrs. and Miss, 58, 71, 86, 87
Bath, 11, 13, 14, 19, 35, 53, 54, 61,
  62, 63, 69, 74, 98, 112
Beaumont, Sir G. and Lady, 110,
  112, 128
Belfield House, Wyke Regis, 89,
  103, 128, 150, 166 (Note 3, Ch. 8)
Bellas, Mrs., 15, 17, 39
Bembridge, I.o.W., 79, 80, 83
Bennet, Jane, 55, 59
— *Elizabeth*, 131, 132, 133

187

Index

Index

Index

Price, Mr., 149
— Mrs., 78
— *William*, 36, 137, 139, 140, 142
— *Fanny*, 36, 56, 78, 137, 138, 140, 142, 143, 149, 152
Pyrenees, 127

Q

Quillinan, Edward, 68, 156, Note 5, 163

R

Racedown, Dorset, 29, 30, 34, 35, 37, 38, 50
Ramsgate, Kent, 75, 77, 135
Reynolds, Frederick, 57, 58
Richmond, Surrey, 40, 94
Robinson, John, 27, 28, 60, 125
— Mrs., 60, 125
Routhedge, Mr., 99
Russell, Lady, 20, 43, 44, 45, 64, 65, 114, 115
Rydal Mount, 162, Note 3, Ch. 5

S

Sanders, Mrs., 144
Sandown, I.o.W., 144
Seymour, Mr., 75
Sidmouth, 17
Shakespeare, 26, 55, 56, 57, 82, 126, 129, 130
Shambles, The, 24, 101, 102, 110, 116
Shanklin, 79, 80
Sharp, William, 163, Note 5, Ch. 5
— Granville, 163, Ch. 5, 5
Sharp, Anne, Miss, 54, Note 5, 5, 163
Slyfield House, Gt. Bookham, 93
Sockburn, Yorks., 30
Sotherton, 56
Southampton, 13, 48, 52, 107
Southey, Robert, 80, 151
Spedding, Mrs., 27, 28, 35, 132
— John, 27, 28
— Maria, 27, 28, 35
— Margaret, 27, 28, 35
Spenser, 26, 82
Squibb, G. D., 166, Note 3, Ch. 8
Staple Inn, 28, 29, 31, 40, 48, 74, 75

Starcross, 17
St. Boniface House, 11, 79, 80, 81, 83, 150, 151, 153
St. Boniface Down, 11, 80, 83, 154
Steventon, Hants., 12, 13, 14, 15, 16, 17, 37, 54
— Rectory, 11, 12, 38, 52, 53, 54, 57, 62, 156
Stoneleigh, Warwicks, 12
Switzerland, 12, 19, 94

T

Teignmouth, 15, 52
Temple Sowerby, 30
Thorpe, John, 56
Threlkeld, Elizabeth, 27
Thrush, The (ship), 140
Tilney, Henry, 35, 36, 56
— *Eleanor*, 56
Tintern Abbey, 143
Tonbridge, 12
Torbay, 35, 37, 38

U

Uppercross, 34, 65, 69, 114, 118
Usk (river in Mon., Wales), 126

V

Vallon, Annette, 31, 48, 49, 50, 107, 135, 149
— Caroline, 31
Vaudracour and Julia, 107
Ventnor, I.o.W., 80, 150, 151

W

Wales, 17, 126, 127, 155, 156
Walter, Mrs., 52
Welby, Mrs., 67
Weller, Captain and Rosina, 150
Wentworth, Captain Frederick, 20, 21, 22, 25, 39, 43, 44, 46, 61, 62, 63–66, 70, 71, 76, 84, 108–12, 116–18, 123, 125, 127, 130
West Indies, 26, 77
Weston, Mr., 72, 73
— *Mrs.*, 58, 72, 73, 74

191

Index